Advance Praise

"This is a must-read for anyone who wants a forever relationship without making the same mistakes they did in their past ones. *Untangling* is *the* guide for letting go—a roadmap to a confident and open-hearted future."
—**Jack Canfield and Kimberly Kirberger**, *#1 New York Times Best-selling Authors of the Chicken Soup for the Soul Books*

"Unapologetically raw, *Untangling* is the message everyone needs to discover. A journey of heartbreak, self-reflection and self-love can be hard, but if you keep your heart open it can never be broken. This book is a gem . . . a spiritual and emotional gift to everyone who reads it and decides to take action to rise up in their lives."
—**Logan Lester**, *Miss Texas USA 2018*

"*Untangling* is a vulnerable reminder that a breakup does not mean you're broken. Emma's flawless way of describing her pain will resonate with anyone who has ever been blindsided by a tragic ending. A beautiful journey of self-discovery after heartache, the realization that healing isn't linear and that people aren't always capable of giving us what we deserve. We are privy to her innermost thoughts and through her courageous transparency we receive a gift— seeing her growth outweigh her pain and remembering that we are capable of that too."

—**Danni Starr**, *National Media Personality and Author of Empathy and Eyebrows - A Survivalist's Stories on Reviving Your Spirit After Soul-Crushing Sh*tstorms*

"*Untangling* is an invaluable addition to Emma's *Life Letters* series. The book is honest, raw and undeniably soothing to a reader's heart. It is layered with life lessons on how to move on, with honest confessions of love and the importance of taking the journey from heartbreak to healing. Starting at the end, the book unwinds in a unique way, revealing important messages about what it feels to love, to hurt, to break your heart and to move on. I absolutely love Emma's healing words and I tune into them daily. This is a writer who is here to soothe hearts all over the world and teach the importance of self-love."

—**Ruby Dhal**, *Speaker, Performer, and Author of 'My Hope for Tomorrow'*

"*Untangling* is a great reminder of the *many* things that are important for the soul. It reminds me I am not the only one who's going through heartache, struggling to find answers to questions for which there are often none. This book helped me stop blaming myself—and find a way forward with a new hope for love. Thank you Emma Grace for helping me understand, and for giving me a new perspective on this life. Thank you for being brave enough to share your story and writing this beautiful book. We love you."

—**Sabina Meisinger**, *Thai TV Host*

"Through self-worth, humility, and charm . . . Emma's *Untangling* is the good friend you need during one of life's most challenging moments . . . a broken heart."

—**Cyndal Gilmore**, *Hamilton Cast Member*

Untangling

THE LIFE LETTERS

Untangling

Starting at an Ending
to Find a Beginning

Emma Grace

NEW YORK

LONDON • NASHVILLE • MELBOURNE • VANCOUVER

Untangling

Starting at an Ending to Find a Beginning

Published in New York, New York, by Morgan James Publishing. Morgan James is a trademark of Morgan James, LLC. www.MorganJamesPublishing.com

ISBN 9781631950131 paperback
ISBN 9781631950148 eBook
Library of Congress Control Number: 2020931383

Cover & Interior Design by:
Christopher Kirk
www.GFSstudio.com

Author Photography by:
Jacadra Young

Morgan James is a proud partner of Habitat for Humanity Peninsula and Greater Williamsburg. Partners in building since 2006.

Get involved today! Visit
MorganJamesPublishing.com/giving-back

For Lindsey, who walked *with* me towards a beginning.

A Note from the Author

This is a book for all the hearts who were once *in love*, who are falling *out* of love, or who will one day be *head over heels in love* again. As you're reading it, I want you to remember, amidst *all that other stuff* you're going crazy thinking about—*that it is not your fault.*

I mean it. It's not.

It is *not your fault* that you can't see through eyes of love and eyes of reason at the same time. It's not your fault if you fall in love too early—or fell out of love too late. It's not your fault if you can't make it work. Or tried too hard to make it work. Or if you can't or won't or weren't able to see that maybe they didn't *totally deserve* what you ended up giving them—or how long you gave it to them for. It is not your fault if you messed up how it was supposed to go—if you called too much or texted too much because you loved them *that* much. You aren't needy. You aren't weak. You were just—*in love.* And that, no matter what, is a beautiful thing.

We are not supposed to predict things in this life. We are just supposed to live them. And experience them. And learn from them. So I want you to know, no matter where you are on this journey—that *it is not your fault*, how it all goes. You are part of a much larger constellation of experiences that ultimately shape what happens to you. And sure, a small part you'll get the chance to steer—to choose—but the rest will be totally and completely out of your hands.

Love is, well, it's a beautiful mess—and it *always* will be.

I don't mean that in a bad way, though.

What I mean is—we're all out there trying and searching and loving and losing and healing and hurting and breaking. All of us. We have *all* been hurt. And we will *all* be loved.

Maybe you find your *one* when you're in the sixth grade. Or maybe they will stumble into your life at a time you didn't even believe in love anymore. But that's how it works. All of it. You need the uncertainty. You need the one who breaks you *and* the one who builds you. You need the one that loves you like crazy when you're not ready to be loved like crazy—and especially the one *you* love like crazy—who just isn't ready for you.

You need to trust and be trusted, break and be broken. You need to feel that powerful, eyes-across-the-room kind of passion—and you need to know what a *partner* feels like, too. The one who won't just kiss you like you've never been kissed—but who will see your beauty in the messy-haired mornings and want to be there—*want* to be there—when you're sick. And hurt. And insecure. And stressed. And, well—for *all those other things* life throws at us after the photo-op and Instagram post and beachy sandy picture part of the love story fades away.

Because it does. It *always* does.

Love isn't always shiny. It's not always starry eyes and holding hands. It's not always forever. Love is learning. And growing. And patient. And deep. It's a kiss goodnight even when they're mad at you. Someone who doesn't think a fight is the end. It's the one who answers your calls and is patient through your chaos—the one who listens and watches and waits. So while you're out there trying to figure it all out, just do me one favor. Count all these experiences you're having—*even the ones you don't want*— as stepping stones. As a foundation. As an essential part of your journey. Because *each* one, love—each one—brings you that much closer.

To real.

So if you remember nothing else from the beginning or the middle or the end of your love stories—and there *will* be more love stories—remember this:

It is ok to forgive yourself for *all the things you did* when love was leading you.

with love.

**

Let's Break It Down Like This

How to Read This Book

What I really want to do is tell you what this book *isn't*. But first, I know I have to tell you what it *is*. So, let me do that. *This* is a book that starts at an ending. To find a beginning.

I use the word "untangling" for that.

But—you might call it breaking up. Or ending a relationship. Or getting a divorce. Or one of nine *million* other things that label the end of our love stories. And you know, in simply writing that—that this book is about endings—I feel like I am doing you a complete disservice. Because that is *most certainly* not *just* what this book is about.

And if you're browsing through the shelves at some book store—or scanning this online—I don't want you to think that this book isn't for you just because you're not *in* that place right now. You're happy in your life—in your relationship—and so when you read what I just wrote, maybe you end up putting this book down. Take it off your list. Say, *that's not for me.* Because, well, you don't *need* to reflect on endings right now, right?

Oh, love—*wrong*.

Whether you're facing an ending right now or not—I'll bet you can at least admit that you've been through your fair share. Some of them you understand well, and others—they probably still tuck you into bed at night. Don't they? With questions. With hurt. With unresolved feelings. Maybe—even with a little regret. And so that, coupled with the simple truth that all of us will face endings throughout our lifetimes—way more often than we'd like, and certainly more than we ever prepare ourselves for—is what brings me to my point.

The ending is never the story. But the ending *is* often what leads us *to* the story.

And so *that* is what this book is about.

The story of what comes next.

And about being stuck in the middle. And self-growth. And reflection. But it's also a book about finding happiness. And looking back just long enough to move forward. It's about *learning* from your experiences instead of just having them. And mostly—this is a book about how to discover who you are when *you are with* other people—and what you choose to do with that.

So I'm just going to say this. To you. About *how* to read this book:

If you're facing an ending right now, then start at the beginning. And read it all the way through. Or—if you're a few weeks or months in, and struggling with whether to call or whether it was your fault or whether they miss you—then skip directly to those chapters. And read them over and over and over. Underline words. Earmark pages. Use this book as a journal. A good friend. A guide. And you do it, love, until you know— and are confident in—the choice you want to make. For you. And lastly, if you're in a committed relationship—then I encourage you to read this as both a reflection *and* a growth opportunity. Not because you think in any way that your current relationship is headed toward an end— but rather, because you accept that endings in love are inevitable. And you've had them. And you will probably have them again. Read this book because you want to explore yourself. And your past. And you *are ready* to start harnessing the incredible power of knowing *who you are* when *you are with* other people.

So, read it however you need to read it. But I encourage you to read it.

And I promise you, after you do, you're going to be armed with some pretty valuable tools. And all of them—love, *all of them*—come in the form of self-awareness. You're going to come out of reading this knowing *a lot more* about who you are. And how you respond to situations. And types of people. And why you pick the people you pick. And make the choices you do in love. You're going to come out of this knowing a little more about what you want. And what you will and won't accept. And what you expect from others. And how love changes you. And what endings and beginnings look like in your life.

I hope I will make you laugh. And smile. And reflect. But mostly, think. And so maybe that's the best place to stop for now. Right at the beginning.

**

1. The Beginning

A few things to get us started.

T hey say you should use your journey. So I am going to. And I want to begin with a confession: I am *bad* at breakups. I'll get to what I actually mean by "breakups" in a minute. But I just want to start by saying it's *really* hard to write that. It's hard to even *admit* it. And—as uncomfortable as it makes me to write—especially in a book that will find itself in countless hands I both know and don't—I am still going to do it. And I will because I believe—I have always believed—that the things that are hard to talk about are the only things that are *ever* worth writing about. I also know—when I go back to edit this—that I will *for sure* read these words with new eyes. Which means, I will also *probably* feel incredibly compelled to cut the raw details out. I know I'll be sitting there in the final editing phase, hovering anxiously over the delete key—with these first few chapters completely highlighted. And all I'll be doing is weighing.

The value of being real. Against the fear of being vulnerable.

These first few chapters—they are going to walk us both through the beginning of an ending. When it's real and vulnerable and messy. When we don't have bumper-sticker quotes to get us through. When we don't get it right. When all we have is a crumbling reality, some big lessons to learn, and a massively broken heart. And you know, I'll want to cut these details out *not* because they aren't an important part of the story, but because—like all of us—I'll want to protect myself.

From you. From what—*you*—will think of my story.

But I am starting this whole book by making myself a promise. That I will *not* do that. And the reason is simple, even if it's hard. I am going to write what is hard for me to write because—during the times in my life I have really struggled, I have often stumbled upon words from other writers who have made me feel like they were writing my story. Simply because they had the courage to write theirs.

And *that* is what I want to do for you. I want to *talk about* the parts of life that are *hard* to talk about. And in doing so, show you how intertwined our stories really are. They may start and end a little differently—and may span different lengths of time and space—but at the core, we are *all the same* in love. We want it. We put our hearts out there. We trust the people we hand them to. And in the end, we either get what we're looking for—or we learn.

And *that* is what this is about. So, contrary to the title of this chapter—like any good breakup story, we don't start at the beginning. We start at the end.

Here goes.

The things that are **hardest to talk about**
are the *only* things
that are ever worth writing about.

**

So—if I were to take a guess, I'd guess that you are smack-dab in the middle of the overanalyzing part, right? Well before acceptance, and maybe even before pain—an ending just simply makes you *think*. Way. Too. Much. You get into this spin of overanalyzing *every single word* that was said. At any point. In any conversation. You go back and look for signs of things you didn't see but think you should of. You reread text messages. You seesaw back and forth between "I absolutely don't deserve this," and "This was *totally* my fault." You get mad that it's happening—that someone you trusted could do this to you. To *what you had*. And then, inevitably, you give yourself a pep talk, pull yourself together, put on a brave face (even when you are absolutely in knots inside) and tell yourself there *must* be something you can learn from this. Right? Like—*that* wasn't your person. And—you *don't want* anyone who doesn't want you.

Sure. And maybe that lasts for a bit.

But then the *moments* happen, don't they? The ones you knew full well were *going* to happen but somehow still seem to blindside you anyway. You pass the coffee shop you used to go to *together.* You have to deal with that *thing* they always used to help you with. *That* day on the calendar comes. You get mail addressed to the two of you. You see the place they used to put their keys—or the absence of their phone charger hanging by *their* side of the bed. Or—maybe it's as painfully simple as having to *say it out loud*. And explain why they aren't coming. And won't be.

And *that* is when it happens.

That strength you were doing so incredibly well with crumbles into a million little pieces. And you do what I *think* we all do but never talk about:

You go back.

You go back and start thinking *it wasn't that bad*. You go back and start telling yourself there *was* love there. They *were* good to you. There were some *incredibly* good times. It's like—you just try to erase the ending— the part where everything fell apart (and why)—and you rewind to the place you were last comfortable in. The place that was *good*. The place that made you—happy.

And *that* is the place where an ending starts getting complicated, isn't it? Because there *were* good times. A lot of them. And you *had* a connection, didn't you? And you were *planning* things. And you *trusted* them. And they made you *feel* something you hadn't felt before.

Oh, love. I get it. I get it *so much more* than I have ever wanted to get it.

But this place—the one where it seems so much easier to go back than to move forward—is the place *so many of us* make a decision that changes the course of our whole lives without even knowing it. I mean, sure— there are, I am certain, so many circumstances where *maybe we should* go back. To fight for the person we love—who loved us. And just as equally—there are so many times we should walk ourselves away without ever looking back. And the trouble with that decision is that we are often forced to make it when we are all clouded with emotion. And so, we're sitting there, alone on our couches or curled up in our beds with tears in our eyes, figuring out whether to move forward or go back without any real facts. Without any clarity. Without giving it the *time* we *all* know we need to give it, but don't want to. When our hearts are shouting go back—but our heads shout even louder *just think about it*.

Now, only you can ever decide what is right for you and your life.

But we're going to talk about a few things in this book that will hopefully help you decide. About how all this feels. About the lies your heart tells you when it's broken. About *how* and *when* to get rid of those things that constantly remind you of that person. About how to make the shift away from what *has happened*—and toward what *is happening*. So you don't get stuck in a place where you can't totally move forward but you can't totally go back. And then, we're going to end with what you need to take away from this. And what part you decide to carry forward with you.

Look, love. You and I are going to talk through a lot of how this is going to go. And through these pages, I am going to repeat one thing over and over and over. Hopefully you'll understand it by the last page, even if you don't at the first. But—*it ended for a reason*. It did. Now, whether that's a *forever thing* or a *just for now* thing, only time will tell. But that's not really what you need to be focusing on right now, anyway. Because the truth you can't deny (and really need to accept) is that, no matter what, it *did* end. And so, something *was* broken if one of you (or both of you) felt the need to end it rather than work through it.

Sometimes people need to grow separately before they can come together. And sometimes your love story is going to end in the middle of the *love* part for no other reason than it just did. And you are going to have to learn to accept that. As hard as it is.

So I'm going to tell you how it has felt for me, and what I have learned, in the hopes my journey helps you on yours. And to be completely honest with you, I am sitting here starting this book in a coffee shop (the same one he and I frequented). It's a Sunday. Two days after someone I thought I knew *so well* looked at me with eyes I didn't even recognize and said he was *done*. For no reason at all. And I'm telling you—it's raw. It stings. I'm still making sense of it. Three days ago, I thought we were living our best life. And now? Now, I've spent these past two days sitting in my house—plaguing myself with those never-ending thoughts of *why* coupled with *you cannot go back to someone who will do that to you.*

I feel the tightness in my shoulders. The world turns outside my window but seems to have come to a screeching halt for me. I know that may sound dramatic—but I'll also bet a whole bunch of you will completely understand what I mean. Every time I venture out, I see *love*. People holding hands, laughing. Every time I turn on the tv or the radio, *something* reminds me of that person. And like a slap in the face, I am continuously reminded over and over that *it* is over. And so, somewhere in the midst of all of that chaos, that hurt, I started thinking about how we *do* this.

The untangling.

How we spend the hours and days and weeks after what I am going to call—the breakup. Now I realize *you* might call it something different in your world. And maybe you do that because you're still in school and *just starting* to figure out your love story. Or—maybe you're coming out of a ten- or twenty-year marriage with someone you thought was your *grow old together* person. Or—maybe you're healing from someone you've known your whole life, and you're much older than you'd ever thought you'd be—doing this whole starting over thing. So because of all those reasons, I *get* that the word *breakup* might seem so incredibly *small* in comparison to what it *does to us*. To you. Your word might be divorce. Or separation. Or growing apart. But—no matter who you are or what you're navigating—and no matter what you want to call it—we all *have* to do this part, love. Want it or not. Ready or not.

We have *got* to untangle.

And so what does that mean? Well—untangling is the days we don't really talk about and aren't *good* at. The place where *so* many of us cover up how we feel with avoidance and isolation—slumping into a lonely place where we swipe even harder on dating apps and throw ourselves into fitness and do *everything we can* to avoid the feeling of *feeling*. It's the place where we give in to the fact that we're alone and it's our fault and there is just *something wrong with us* because this *keeps* happening. It's the place we swirl around in, dancing with all the things that remind us of a life that isn't ours anymore. The place where we honestly *knew* it was broken but still want to go back to—because loneliness is scary. And endings are scary. And a future we've never met and can't see any part of is *much scarier* than anything we had in our past.

And *that* is the place I want to bring a little light to.

And I'm going to write this book as I navigate it—so it's real. And I'm putting more out there than I ever have before because the way I see it—vulnerability is the *only* foundation we can ever really build anything solid on. It's what we all hesitate to do—to give—because, well, vulnerability is just about as scary as it gets. And vulnerability gives other people the chance to have opinions about *our truths*. And that means we can get hurt. Again. Just by putting *who we are* out there.

So this is the story of how we *do* a part of life we have to do but never wanted to. This is the story of what we learn from experiences we never thought we'd have and lessons we never knew we needed. I know it's going to hurt—but I also know that pain is often what teaches us most about what matters in this life. One day, you will be certain of that, too.

Time is an incredible lens. And until it shows you why things had to happen like they did—just trust that these parts you're living now are all just a powerful way this life is choosing to steer you. As it teaches you, slowly, the beautifully complicated art of untangling your knots.

**

2. "This *Cannot* Be Happening."

When it all comes crumbling down.

Things had been different for a few days. Suddenly. Unexpectedly. You know—I'll just say it came from completely out of the blue. And from where I sat, nothing had *happened*. We hadn't been fighting, there were no big life events plaguing us, we didn't have things we were "working through," there was no—*anything*—that would explain what had changed. Or why. And to be honest, the change wasn't anything I could quite put my finger on, exactly—I guess you could just call it a change in *energy.*

Now, side note—I'm firmly convinced that some people can just *sense* things. Call it a gut feeling. Call them empaths. Call it plain old intuition. But whatever it is—sometimes it's a helpful superpower. And others, it's just *not.* When you *feel* things like that, you can often sense something happening before the person feeling it is even *aware* they are feeling it. And trust me, that is *not* always an easy thing to wrestle with. You flip-flop back and forth between talking about it and making it real—or not talking about it, and letting it eat you up inside.

11

But anyway, *something* about how his eyes caught mine just seemed—*off.* Like he was hiding something. And what seemed crazy to me, is this change appeared right after some of the best times we'd spent together. When the rest of the world disappears and it's just you and that other person standing in time. When words are said that bubble up feelings of *yes* and *trust* and *maybe this is how it's supposed to be.* Those are the times you *can't* see it coming. Endings. Because your eyes are completely clouded with the beginning or the middle of what you hope and pray is your incredible love story.

I thought we had been *really* good at communication, and so I figured he would let me know when he was ready. So, I gave him time.

He pulled back slowly. First it was the delay in responding. Then it was the wishy-washy level of commitment that settled more in the *maybe* zone than the outright yes or no zone. Then it was his tone. I remember asking him over the course of a week or so if everything was alright. And rather than opening up about whatever *it* was that was bothering him, he started to snap a little.

"You *always* ask me that. You always think something is going on."

Now, just another little side note here: I'm also firmly convinced that when people use the word *always*, there is usually *always* something actually going on. *Always* is a word that comes from a place of frustration. A word we use as an amplifier—to strengthen and intensify a point we are usually trying *way too hard* to make.

Anyway, him pulling back, coupled with the lack of any substantive communication about why, is where I knew something was really wrong.

And I guess that's the place we all start measuring, isn't it? Once we *feel* that something is happening—especially in the absence of any concrete information telling us why—we start hyperfocusing on *every single* little detail. And we collect these details from every interaction we have— or every lack of interaction—while we try with everything we've got to figure out what is happening *before* it actually happens. We start paying attention to how long it takes *that* person to respond to messages they used to immediately respond to. Whether they answer on the first or ninth ring. Or not at all. We are *constantly* sensing whether the connection is still there that used to carry us. And the longer we go without those things—or with fundamental *changes* in those things—the more we get in our own heads.

And overthinking is a dangerous game. Because that's the place the chaos starts.

When we get into that spin of overthinking and overanalyzing, then *we* also change how we act in (or react to) a situation. We don't see that part happening, of course, because we're just focused on what the other person is doing. And how *that* is affecting us. But when *we* change how we act; *they* change how they act. And it's a vicious cycle. Where one side is contributing to the other, and the spinning just keeps getting faster and faster and faster until we have *each* created a story about what is happening, and why.

A story we haven't communicated to each other.

A story that is likely *very* far from the real truth.

A story that, with each word we write, cracks a little more of the foundation we have spent so long building our love story on.

Anyway, the point came where I couldn't *wait* to figure it out anymore. So, I called him. I was kind. Genuine. Not argumentative. And he was— immediately cold. Like, cold in a way I'd never seen in him before. Still thinking this was something we could work through, I explained that things had *felt* different, and I wasn't sure why. I asked if he felt it too. I *tried* to get him to talk to me—I mean, we'd spent *hours* and *hours* talking about everything we could in this life. Even communication itself, and how *incredibly hard* it could be when *things* actually did get hard.

"I guess so," he confessed. "I mean, we haven't talked as much as usual."

I ask him again to tell me what is going on. He reverts back to diversion.

"You *always* think something is wrong. Nothing is wrong." (See what I mean about *always*?)

I calmly point out that there is clearly something wrong because we'd never spoken like this to each other before.

"Things are fine," he snaps. "They're *fine*." (Uh-oh. *Fine*. The other danger word.)

"Can we meet up tonight? Talk about this in person?" I ask.

When
you overthink,
you change how you
act in, or react to, a situation.
And when *you* change how *you* act—
they change how *they* act.
**And *that* is how the
spinning begins.**

He mumbles something about being tired and "not wanting to get into all this right now," (All this?) but agrees to meet up. In my mind, we were going to see each other and talk through this *thing* that was happening that I didn't understand and seemed to have no apparent cause. In my head, things were going to be ok.

Things were *not* ok.

He met me in the courtyard near my house. He was leaning against a concrete wall, and when he saw me walking toward him, he turned his head away. *Away.* He had his arms folded across his chest protectively—closed off. All I can say is—it was really, really surreal. *Weird,* even. I know, not quite an eloquent phrase for a writer, but, alas. I mean, I guess I was still expecting him to be *him.* The person I *thought* I knew so well. The person that just *days ago* was talking about us and trust and how excited he was for the future. The person whose eyes had started to feel like home. And I'm telling you, there was *none* of that there. None of it. And it's almost cliché to say, but when I tell you he looked like a stranger, I *cannot* stress it enough. I literally did not *know* the person I was looking at.

I walked up to him and he looks at me.

I force a smile. "Can I get a hug?" I ask.

He doesn't say anything, but stands up like it takes all the effort in the world. And he one-arm hugs me. (Ugh). I remember searching his eyes in that moment and silently pleading with him to open back up. To *look* like the person who had been *my* person just days ago.

That person was not there.

As we walked down the street, I could sense that all around me, people were heading excitedly into their Friday evenings. And then there was me. Walking next to a stranger.

I had been cast into some parallel universe where everything was falling apart at a time I had thought things were finally all coming together. I was walking next to a stranger that used to hold my hand. That used to laugh with me. That just the Friday before—was telling me I could trust him. And I should. But this stranger—he was responding to my sentences with one-word answers. For every question I asked, I got nearly silence. He literally offered *nothing* as input or answers or reasons. And the longer I looked at this person I had known so well—that I *thought* I had truly cared about—the longer it took to see him. Who was this? This closed-off, *cold,* passive-aggressive anchor that was dragging us both down at the same time?

We stopped walking and sat on these cold gray stairs on this side street in my neighborhood that I don't think I'll ever look the same way at again. During the first part of the conversation—if you can even call it that—he did really well to hold up the "You always read into things" and "nothing is wrong" story. But as time ticked by, he admitted that "maybe he'd been thinking about some things," and "maybe he just didn't *know* anymore."

My. Absolute. Most. Favorite. Break. Up. Lines. Ever.

Now. I feel like, in hindsight, this was a learning moment. So I'll tell you—when someone doesn't *know* how they feel, then I'm sorry, love, but *the answer is no.* Unequivocally. Totally. No. I *think* most of us realize that in the rational part of our brains. But when we're in the midst of the *I can't believe this is happening* moment, we don't always act with self-respect at the forefront of our decision making. It's human.

I started getting frustrated with his lack of contribution to the conversation. His coldness. And so anger begins to take over the place concern used to be.

"So are you telling me your feelings have changed completely in a matter of—*days*? Because I'm pretty sure a few *days* ago, *you* were the one pulling *me* forward."

He mutters another "I don't know." And like—completely shuts down. I sat there looking at this person and it honestly felt like I was living someone else's life. I remember asking over and over, out loud and to myself, *what is happening right now?* I just totally didn't understand where all this was coming from. So suddenly. So completely without some sort of catalyst that I could identify. Something to—make sense of it all.

But something clearly had changed for him.

And I don't think I will ever know what it was—because despite all the *words* he had said about how much this had meant to him; *this person* didn't even think I deserved the respect of an explanation. After a few more questions from me, followed by a few more *one-word* passive-aggressive answers from him, he stood up, and said, and I quote, "I'm done. I'm out."

And he walked himself away from me. No goodbye. No looking back.

Just left me sitting on those cold concrete steps.

And this is the part that is hard to write, especially when I spend my life talking to you about the importance of self-respect. But I'm going to write it anyway. I'm going to tell you. And I'm going to do it because I promised you I'd be real.

I was so incredibly shocked by what was happening and *still* not under-standing any part of the why—that I got up and I *walked after him.* I walked after the man whose back was facing me as he walked away from all the words he said he'd meant. The man who had offered me nothing in the conversation. Who had ended a relationship with "I'm out." (What is that?) I walked after the man who was burning something down with no kindness and no maturity and absolutely no respect. I totally should have had some witty *have a good life* comment. I totally should have picked myself up and walked bravely in the opposite direction with my head held high.

But, I didn't—and I give myself a pass for that. Because I cared about him. And I was confused. And frankly, yes, hurt and not ready to let it all go. *Especially* when I didn't understand it.

I called his name. And—he *literally* did not even turn around.

I called it again. No response.

I walked faster.

When I caught up to him, I linked my arm with his in an effort to slow him down—and asked one final time. "*What* is happening right now? Why are you doing this? Why won't you just tell me what is going on?"

His arm stiffened and he looked at me again coldly—and just said one last time—"I have nothing else to say. I'm done. I'm out." And that man got in his car, slammed the door, and left me standing there watching him drive away.

If they don't *know* how they feel—
then I'm sorry, **but the answer is no.**

And that is how it ended. Like *that.*

Now, just for context, I'm going to give you some additional details. I've been in my fair share of relationships. Most of them have lasted *years.* This one was not even close to that. We weren't married. We didn't live together. We didn't have kids or joint bank accounts. And I guess that's why it's sort of ironic that something like this—*like him*—could prompt me to write an entire book. But life is like that, isn't it? And since love is not some neat little mathematical equation—it doesn't really have to make sense, does it?

I tell you this because I want you to know that how *long* you are together doesn't really much matter, other than to predict how *many* knots there will be left to untangle in the end. And I want you to know that—while our *experiences* are generally unique, *we* are not. Humans are so very much the same at the core—especially when it comes to love and loss. A relationship can be short and intense—or it can be long and intense. And intense can mean good things. Or bad things. Relationships can fizzle out quickly—or slowly unravel over the course of an entire decade. They can be complicated. Or perfect. Or confusing. They can move fast. Or *so* incredibly slow. And sometimes, they can be all of those things at once.

So maybe you're dealing with a broken heart you got from your high school sweetheart. Maybe you're breaking up after three months. Or three years. Or maybe, even three decades. Maybe you're sitting there, alone, looking at this world and not recognizing it at all—because without *them*, you have truly known no other life. Or maybe you've been trying to leave for years—knowing it wasn't healthy but couldn't quite let go. Maybe it was kids. Or finances. Or family. Or health. Or—one of a million other *really* complicated reasons I'm not even going to pretend to understand. The nuances are always going to vary, love, but I think the rest of it—the *feelings* part? Those are mostly the same. And that's the part I want to explore.

How you felt. And what you did with all that.

Anyway—just to round out this story, I need to share how it *really* ended. The next morning (like, less than twelve hours later)—when I was still reeling from what had happened and thinking he'd definitely call to say he'd made a mistake—*he* was already back on the dating site we'd met on. (Yes, I checked. Yes, dating apps are the bane of *everyone's* existence. Yes, we are all still hoping we'll run into the person of our dreams in the broccoli aisle.).

And *this* is the world we're supposed to find love stories in. *This* is how someone who said they cared about me responded to—um, I *still* don't even know what happened. Maybe it was something I did but will never know. Maybe something crazy was going down in his life that he just couldn't share with me. But I'll tell you—no matter what the reason was, I keep going back to one simple truth. He *could* have chosen to talk to me about it. And he didn't.

And that is what grounds me right now.

**

So this is the moment it all starts. The untangling. And I tell you all those little details because I want to be real with you. I *promised* I'd be real with you. I mean, I almost want you to feel like you just read a part of my diary. Or you overheard me talking to my best friend. And I want you to feel that way because I know that *self-help* books sometimes have a stigma. And maybe the reason that stigma develops is because *most* of the time, they can seem sort of, *textbook*. Cold. Hard to apply.

And it probably doesn't help that generally, when we arrive at the place where we actually *need* self-help books, things are already tough. We're already struggling. And so when we start reading, we find the *do this* and *try that* doesn't really come with any significant *context* about how it all feels. In the beginning. In the middle. When we haven't quite figured out how to heal *or* grow. And we're just treading water in the middle of a hurricane trying our best not to drown. So the way I see it, maybe we don't need the roadmap as much as just the *validation* that it's ok to feel the way we do.

However that is. At the beginning of the growth journey.

So, let me just start by telling you what I know you need to hear. *Everything is going to be ok.* It will be. I promise. And I also want you to know that *one day* you're going to forgive yourself. For what you did. Or didn't do. For how you feel. Or didn't feel. We all make mistakes, love. We all act with our hearts first. We all hold on a little too long and a little too hard sometimes. And sure—we all eat a few lies when our hearts are hungry. That's just how it works.

And look—I know my story isn't your story. I also know that some of you will read this and say—she thinks *that* was hard? *Please.* And you know, I'm going to give you that freedom to decide how you will judge my story. Well—at least the part I'm sharing. But I honestly hope that's not the angle you'll take. Because *how* we get there is not the story I'm writing. It's the *beginning* of the story I'm writing. And truth be told, the *how* is always going to be different. I mean, like we just talked about— maybe you got completely blindsided by someone you thought was your forever. Maybe you know *exactly* why it ended. Maybe you could have fixed it, but didn't want to. Maybe you contributed to it—or it was out- right your fault. Maybe it happened so slowly you didn't even see it until it was already done. Maybe you're coming out of a twenty-year marriage or emerging after your very first breakup. And I'm not going to pretend to know the details of what you're carrying, love. But I do know that, unfortunately, most of us are going to experience a whole bunch of different *kinds* of endings. Some that will make sense. Others that just won't. And whether we have all the information we need to understand, or we don't, the next step is always the same.

Figuring out how to move forward *without* the need to go back.

And maybe that's just one of those great simple truths. One that takes a lifetime to really understand. But the way I see it? Moving forward is that beautifully complex art of what we choose to do *after* we learn something we never really wanted to know in the first place. It's how we teach ourselves to walk alone again, without the hand that spent so long holding ours next to us. It's choosing to *feel* it rather than finding something to *avoid* feeling it. It's teaching ourselves to look back at what happened. And learning from it—but not lingering on it. Not dwelling on it. Not burying it. And I'll tell you, love, mostly—it's what we choose to tell ourselves *about* what we learned in the days and weeks and months that come after.

Because *that* is where *what we went through* gets its label as a lesson. Or as a scar.

And *that* is the real story. What *we do* with what happens *to us*.

So, no matter how you got here, here you are. At the place where the healing begins.

**

Moving forward
is that beautifully complex art
of what we choose to do
after we learn something
we never really wanted to know
in the first place.

3. "I Do *Not* Deserve This."

What you tell yourself at the beginning.

I'm just going to say it right now. And get it completely out of the way. You're going to tell yourself *a lot* of things in the beginning. In those hours—days—weeks—after any kind of an ending, your mind is—and I'm sorry for this—but, it's going to drive you completely insane. It's going to *plague* you with *what ifs*. It's going to churn incessantly during any moment you don't keep it completely focused on something else. You're going to *spend so much time* overthinking and overanalyzing what happened that you're *legitimately* going to start wishing your mind came with an off switch.

I get it. But it's the early stages, love. And these are the hardest—when you seesaw constantly between *how* and *why*.

When I walked home that night, after he had literally driven away and left me standing on that curb, I remember thinking through this space I was living in now. I mean, in reality—I was standing in *my* same world but—somehow, it looked like a completely different place. One I didn't *know* anymore. That didn't make *sense* to me. It was a Friday. I was supposed to be excited for the weekend. We were supposed to be going places and doing things. Relaxing. Laughing. Dreaming. Building. And you know, before I had come down to meet him in that courtyard, I had thrown away the last wilting flower from the bouquet he had brought me the week before "for no reason at all." That's some crazy irony, huh?

Anyway, I thought about what this new place meant and whether—even if he were to come back with more answers somewhere down the road—I could *ever* see him through the same eyes again. And for that moment, the answer was no. A hard no. Because—in those first few hours after this truth started to set in, I *felt* with absolute certainty that I *did not ever want someone who could treat me like that to hold such an important place in my life.*

I did not deserve this.

And whether I did something—or I didn't—to contribute to how he was feeling, he *always* had the choice to communicate that. And he chose *not to*. And even more than simply choosing not to—he chose to treat me in a way that caused me to literally look at his face—into his eyes—and see a completely different person standing there.

I did *not* want that. I was sure of it.

That absolute certainty is always my initial phase post-breakup. Maybe it's shock. Maybe it's because I haven't yet had time to process what it all means just yet. Maybe it's because reconciling two completely parallel realities—how we were supposed to head out of town that weekend and instead I was looking at someone I didn't know that was telling me things

I couldn't understand—takes time. Maybe it's a little bit of both. But that's always my first thought with bad breakups. That I don't *deserve* this. And even more—I don't *want* it.

And you know, maybe that's just life being kind initially—because it knows full well the next morning it's going to sting in a way none of us are ever prepared for. But that's what happens. After I go to sleep that first night—and by sleep, I mean after I toss and turn and wake up to question whether this is really happening *over and over*—I wake up to phase two. And phase two is the complete polar opposite of *I don't deserve this.* Phase two is the *maybe it was all my fault* place. The one where strength is completely gone. Logic and reason are completely gone. And now, the job of healing becomes piecing together what it means to be in this new world where you are—*without* that person. And I'm not sure why, but this is usually the time we blame ourselves for some, or all, of what happened.

But we'll get to that.

Look, I've already broken this news to you, but—when your heart is hurting, your mind is *not* your friend. I'm sorry for that. But—it's just one of those unfair little yin and yang conundrums of this crazy old world. While your mind struggles to understand, it's going to seek answers to questions that might not *actually have* answers. Or at least not *easy* ones. And in that lack of clarity, it is going latch on to whatever information it can find, and try to construct a story to tell you. Even if what *it* knows— isn't—enough to build the story.

You understand that, right?

For me, I had actually started to convince myself that *asking him* several times (like, literally, three) over the course of a week *what was wrong* was enough to end the whole relationship. I mean, *maybe* he got frustrated with my questions. *Maybe* I was being too sensitive. *Maybe* there actually wasn't anything wrong and I did this—forcing him to talk about something that wasn't real or he wasn't ready for and it was just—too much.

No. I'm just going to tell you (and remind me) right now—that is *not* a possible story.

You know what *is* a possible story? That me asking him those things *could* have frustrated him. That he might not have *liked* them. Sure. But again, we are all adults here. And he had the opportunity to communicate to me what he needed, so I could change how I was responding to the situation.

And he didn't. So I couldn't. And it broke.

The nuances of how we process these things in our lives that don't go quite as planned are pretty complicated. They just are. And maybe it's because *we* are complicated. And while we constantly bombard ourselves with questions and blame—especially in hindsight—I need you to remember one really important thing here. *Communication is always a choice.* It's where we make and break just about everything in love. And while I'm sure, like in all relationships, there *is* shared blame somewhere—I am just *not* going to take the blame for asking for more information when things felt wrong to me. Someone told me this morning that the only time people get irritated with those types of questions is when something *really is* wrong and they just aren't ready to talk about it yet. That no one *actually* gets irritated with someone for asking if everything is ok out of genuine concern.

Well. That's telling, isn't it?

When we get to the end of a relationship, whether it ends up being mutual or completely one-sided—truth, I'm afraid, is not often the prevalent force. I mean, we all hope that truth is there, somewhere, but the *truth* is, there are way too many emotions and hurt and other motivations that drive the interactions that happen at the end. And so, naturally, things tend to get muddy. And confusing. And when we're in that place, we're vulnerable—and acting more in survival mode than building mode. Which means, we aren't often getting answers. We're just getting words.

So—I know this will be hard. But try your best not to overanalyze the words that came right at the end. They aren't the ones that get to tell the whole story—and they definitely don't get to *retell* the whole story. I mean, sure—you're going to question whether everything that came before the hurt was actually real. You're going to question whether they actually ever really loved you. You're going to question how they could possibly walk away after all you've been through. After all the promises that were made.

And that's all normal, love. *Completely normal.*

Just do me a favor and keep in mind that endings are always confusing. And hard. I mean it. Do your best not to reread their messages over and over and over. And don't analyze the words they used. And compare them to what they used to say. Or how they used to say it. Things aren't usually that transparent. *Or* that simple.

So I'm going to help you refocus. Because there is really *only one truth* here.

It ended.

And that means, for whatever reason, *that* just wasn't your person.

Maybe, like I mentioned before, that status is a *forever* thing. Or maybe it's a *just a right now* thing. But either way, you have *got* to figure out how to move forward right now without going back. And you can blame yourself for whatever you want. You can make it your fault or theirs. You can say it was about an event, or bad timing, or a misunderstanding. But it doesn't much matter. None of that matters. Understanding what happened doesn't change the outcome—and it also doesn't change how *you* need to react to it. We are different people with *each* person we choose to share a portion of our lives with. Which means—*all you can do* is reflect on who you are. And what you choose to do with that.

**

We are different people
with *each* person we choose
to share a portion of our lives with.
So *all you can ever do* is reflect on who you are.
And what you choose to do with that.

A few more things, about this beginning part.

I know you want answers. I know you want them more than anything you've ever wanted. But—*this* just might not be the time for answers. Yeah, I know—that just plain old stinks. It does. But I promise you, love, the answers *will* come. And I also promise you that the answers you're looking for are *not* hiding in the place (or with the person) the questions are coming from. So slow down a little. Try to calm your mind. We're going to work through this. And you *will* come out the other side stronger.

Oh. And you *will* love again. **You will.**

Even though you're hurting like crazy, I want you to keep *that* in your mind *and* in your heart. That you *will love* again. Whether it is them or someone you haven't even met yet—your life will go on. Your heart will move on. And these experiences will all be just an essential part of who you are becoming. So until that all comes together for you, let's just face one truth that is actually worth facing. A truth that will hopefully ground you during this early part—before you make choices that have the potential to hurt you even more.

They stay.

If it's real—and it's healthy—and it was what you both needed—they *stay*.

You can at least believe that, right?

**

The answers
you are looking for
are *not* hiding in the place,
or with the person,
the questions are coming from.

4. "Well, Maybe I *Do* Deserve This."

No, you don't deserve this.

W hat comes next—quite quickly, I might add—is self-doubt. It's actually somewhat ironic that self-doubt follows so closely that surge of strength that initially carried you. And maybe it's just a symptom—one that follows the lack of sleep. The hurricane of emotion. The overanalyzing. The lack of a new message on your phone. The fear that you'll stumble on a photo you *just* can't handle seeing. Or, maybe—all of it—coupled with the realization that you have a daunting job ahead of you:

Fill the next twelve hours. Alone. *Without that person* that used to fill them with you.

And the self-doubt phase—it always seems to start in the morning. The *first* morning. I don't know why that is, exactly—but maybe it's because, after an ending, the morning is never *just* a regular old morning, is it? Mornings are the quiet times you reserve for the people and things the rest of the world doesn't get a chance to see. It's your little circle of trust. Your source of inner balance. Maybe in some ways, the center of your whole world. And because *that* person probably held *a significant* role in your mornings in some way, I guess that kind of makes sense, doesn't it?

How much it hurts.

And so—somewhere in that quiet—the self-doubt finds a crack. And it trickles in. You know what it sounds like. If they could walk away like that—if there was *no part of them* that felt like working through this together was a better option than completely ending it—what does that *say about you?* That you're hard to love? Easy to let go of? Easy to *fall out of love* with? Not—someone *special?* And—even if it was you that ended it, *how come they haven't reached out?* To say they miss you? To try to fix things? To work through it? Did you make a mistake? One that—(and here's the whopper of all things self-doubt)—will cause you to be alone for the rest of your life?

And *that's* just the start of those worries.

I certainly always feel like that. And I'll tell you, in most other parts of my life, I consider myself a *very* independent, confident woman. I try to be strong. To face this world with a good balance of logic and heart. But in these moments, I am, like all of us, reduced to a puddle of *this is all my fault.* And *it must be something that was wrong with me* if someone couldn't love me. I go back to—maybe I don't measure up to the other women he has loved. Maybe I'm not as—*pretty.* Maybe my body isn't good enough. Maybe I'm too set in my ways. Too independent. Not smart enough. Maybe my life isn't as exciting as it should be. Maybe I'm not *fun.* Maybe I wore the wrong clothes. Said the wrong things. Invited him to things too early. Said how I felt too late.

Yes. Once you get on the self-doubt train, you tend to stay on it for a lot longer than you need to.

Don't.

Can we *just* agree as a starting point, that a relationship takes two people? And—if we can accept that truth, then maybe we can also accept that there are always at *least* two sets of emotions and circumstances and realities and truths playing into *everything* that is happening to us at any one time. Which also means—even in those circumstances where a breakup *is* your fault, it is never *entirely* your fault. There are so many interconnected, intertwined, contributing factors that make up a relationship—it's just about impossible to neatly separate out blame from fault.

But we'll come back to that later.

During the self-doubt phase, because it comes so early in the process—*everything* is going to seem hard. It's not that you *can't* do it. Be alone. Live alone. Entertain yourself. Raise your kids yourself. Go back to a life where you're the only driver for your decisions. It's just that—you're not *used* to it anymore. You've gotten used to an *us* on the weekends. An *us* that goes to events. An *us* that is planning a future that no longer exists. And doing life after a breakup means that you have to fundamentally and completely *relearn* almost everything about how your days work.

It's hard.

But, just like it took time to *build* all that—it's also going to take time to *rebuild* from it. You got all tangled up in each other, and this is just the process of untangling the knots. Untangling your life from theirs. And it takes time—and you just need to go in accepting that. And you also need to give yourself permission, right now, to screw it up a little in the process. Because you will. At one point. *Everybody* does.

And—since we're being completely honest here—I do want you to be really cautious of one thing. One important thing. Because in this place, most of us make some critical decisions that we don't even know we are making at the time. Or at least, don't understand the impact of. When we feel how *hard* it is to relearn life on our own, we sometimes decide it's easier to go back than to move forward.

And that is *not* a decision you should make right now.

Do you hear me?

Give. It. Time. Maybe in this early phase—when the sting is still so real—you can talk yourself out of going back pretty easily. Because the part where you *really* miss them and want it all back—that comes later. And much more intensely. But again, we'll get to that.

Just—don't go back. Not right now. When these things happen, we grasp for *anything* that might make the hurting stop. And in our emotional chaos, we somehow even convince ourselves that peace is hiding in the last place we left it. With them.

But trust me, love, *it is not.*

This is the time for healing. *Your* healing. This is the place you *have got* to explore where you are and figure out what you're supposed to learn from it. Your lesson is *not* that you are destined to be alone. It's *not* that you should never trust someone again. And trust me—it *is not* that you should immediately jump into something new because it hurts too much and you just want to make it stop. Well—maybe the hurting part is true. But the way to heal will never be to bury it. Or mask it. Or avoid it. And it *definitely* won't be to put someone new in the place someone else left a hole. You cannot fast-forward this part, love. You cannot skip these first days and weeks. They are critical to your growth. And no matter how it feels right now, there *will* be growth.

Before we get into the rest of this book—which is a little more of a road-map than these first few chapters—I want to talk to you about something I know you're going to struggle with. And this thing—it's something you aren't going to put much stock in right now, given how you're feel-ing—but I still want you to try. I'm talking about your worth. And more specifically, your *self*-worth.

Don't roll your eyes. I mean it.

It's—*so normal.* The comparison. To feel, especially during the hard times, that we just don't measure up. And during those times we strug-gle—it is usually when we need our worth the most, isn't it? The times we really need to draw from our inner strength to protect us from the storms raging around us.

Just like the end of a love story.

The time when we—aren't—somebody's somebody. Or aren't anymore. When we don't have what we want. Or when everything in our lives *is* spinning out of control. Oh, love. I get it. It's so incredibly easy to be in control when you have everything you want. When you have—*them.* Someone you can call or go home to at the end of a long hard day. Some-one who *does* this life with you. Who makes you feel like you matter—and that your life is complete. Whole. Safe. Protected.

But—just like your worth is not higher when somebody loves you—it's also not *lower* when somebody doesn't. I mean, sure—*not* having that person means you might have to figure some stuff out on your own (and you will). It means you might have to pick *yourself* up after a long hard day (and you will). It means you might get your sense of security from somewhere—or something—else (and you will). And that's ok. Do you hear me? That's totally ok. Because when things get hard (or when they *are* hard, like right now), I want you to remember that your worth *is in no way* connected to your ability to be loved. Or the fact that you *are* loved.

Do you get that?

Your worth is never higher—*never higher*—because someone loves you. Or lower because someone didn't. Say that over and over today. Until you believe it.

I mean it.

**

Just—don't go back. Not yet.
When these things happen,
we grasp for absolutely
anything that will make
the hurting stop—
even convincing ourselves
that peace is hiding
in the last place we left it.

So, where are you right now? Bed? Couch? Oh, I know—you would *much rather* just stay in bed right now, because, well—the world just seems *too darn complicated*, doesn't it? Too busy. Too full of—love—for you to even tolerate. The emotional part of you says you can't handle that. But the rational part of you knows you need to. So get up, get dressed, and get out of the house. Even if it's just a walk. Or a few hours with your friends. Or reading a book at a coffee shop. *Around people.* Or, in my case, sitting for the sixth straight hour on this Sunday two days after *my* breakup all went down. Writing this book. (Side note—I'm sure he didn't know he'd get written about like this. But I did warn him. When you know a writer, you *will* eventually get written about. Taylor Swift-style if you do what he did. Wink, wink.)

It might take you forever to get yourself motivated. Maybe it will even seem a heck of a lot easier to just sit there and think. Wallow. Worry. Analyze. Cry. But thinking about the *same things* you've been thinking about over and over—somehow expecting a new truth to help you make sense of it—is just *not* going to happen.

We both know that.

Look—relationships *never* end for one, single, uncomplicated reason. Never. When things break, there are *way* more factors that contribute to getting the two of you to that place. Where ending things becomes the right answer. Or the only answer.

Things did not end because you weren't good enough. Things did not end because you weren't pretty enough. Things did not end because of your body or your words or your hang-ups. Things did not end because you work too hard. Or you don't speak up for yourself. Or your hair is too messy in the morning. Or you spent too much money. Or your skin isn't perfect. Or you can't have kids. Or you don't *want* kids. Or you gained weight. Or you called too much. Or said too much. Or didn't say enough.

Seriously. We *all* need to stop taking responsibility for things that are not *all* our fault. We need to stop thinking we should walk on eggshells around the people we love. We need to stop *ignoring* things that feel wrong just because we're scared of what happens when we say the words out loud. We need to stop thinking that *one single thing* can break a whole entire relationship. I mean it. That's not how it works. If things break because we take our worries or our fears or our insecurities out of our heads and put them into the ears of the people who supposedly love us—is that *really* the kind of love any of us want? And, even more importantly—if *who you are and what you do* breaks a relationship with someone who is supposed to love you, unconditionally, for *who you are and what you do*—is *that* really who you want to spend your life with?

Don't you want someone who listens? Who *wants* to listen? Who accepts you and who you are and what you want? Who grows with you? Complements you? Embraces your faults and loves you *even* when they fundamentally disagree with you? Who says the words when it's easy and *proves them* when it's hard?

Answer those questions for yourself, love, because life *is* hard. And none of us deserve a love story that only grows in the sunshine.

**

This is a hard place to be. And I'm *so* sorry that you have to know how all this feels. I also know you are still missing them like crazy and struggling to make sense of what is happening right now. What *happened* to get you to this place. Alone. Reading *this* book.

And that's why I want you to really focus on what I'm about to tell you. In your world of spinning and chaos—this is something you can latch onto:

People who love each other—or *are working* to love each other—*work through things.*

Read that again.

And then repeat *it* over and over and over. People who are in healthy, *emotionally available* relationships *communicate with each other.* They are able to say when something is bothering them. When they need a little space. When they're having a hard time dealing with something. When *you* are frustrating them. And *why.* They *don't* pull back. They *don't* stop responding to your calls. They don't cheat on you. They don't walk away. They don't end things for some trivial reason they say *you are responsible for.* And they most certainly do *not* blame whatever is happening entirely *on* you.

You cannot shoulder this one on your own. Do you hear me?

Maybe it would help if you thought of relationships like spiderwebs. Strange analogy, I know. But for some reason this works for me. I think we mistakenly like to think of our relationships as these nice, straight little lines—where everything happens sequentially and everything that comes before something else contributes to what comes next. But that is just simply not true. What happened yesterday is not the cause of what happens today. It might be a contributing factor—but it's *never* the out-right cause. This life—and the love stories we weave within it—are much, much more complicated than that. And like a spiderweb, *everything* is connected to something else. In a complicated kaleidoscope of things we can't pick out the ends and beginnings of. Try to understand that.

This is not all your fault.

But trust me, love, it will be your lesson.

**

If who you are and what you do
        breaks a relationship
        with someone who is
        supposed to love you
        unconditionally for
        who you are and what
        you do—then you have
        got to ask yourself, love,
whether *that* was really your person.

5. "Don't You *Dare* Pick Up That Phone."

Wanting the answers only they have.

know where you are right now. I get it. You've probably thought about *every single* possible thing that could have caused or affected or even slightly contributed to the end of your relationship.

And then you rethought about it.

And then you rethought about what you thought about.

And then you felt guilty for thinking about it.

And then you thought about *that,* too, didn't you?

Oh boy. Well. That—coupled with the fact I'm also guessing, since you're missing them like crazy, that you're probably making yourself the bad guy by now—means it's about time to give you some serious context. Because right now, you're stepping into a place that *you think* is just a normal part of healing—and maybe it is, in theory—but it is also what I like to label as *the* danger zone.

The. Danger. Zone.

Because what you *do* in this place changes the course of what happens in the future. I know that might sound like an obvious conclusion—but what I mean is, you're going to *see,* very quickly, the outcome of what you do in this moment. So let me give you some guardrails. This place—it comes *after* you've obsessively talked the whole situation over (and over) with the people you love and trust most. And I'll tell you how you get there. After you've recounted all the details for the twentieth time to people who *weren't there* and are *only going off what you're telling them*—is you start to think that maybe, they have no idea how to actually help you work through this.

And then you start to question how *you* remember things.

And then worse, you start to question whether *how* you remember things—which has now been reinforced by the number of times you've told the story while you've been working through it—was *actually the way things happened*. I mean, the people who love you support *your* side of the story. Generally. And so with each time you talk to one of those people, the story you tell becomes more and more cemented into what you feel is *your truth*. And the story of what *actually* happened gets more and more convoluted. More polarized. More—confusing—as they point out things you didn't see and didn't think about and might not have even wanted to.

Your friends and family are doing their best.

But—to defend you, in some way—they have to *attack* the person who hurt you, don't they? For it to make sense. Which makes you, in your vulnerable emotional state—end up wanting to defend the person who did this to you. It's crazy. How time makes you want to *protect them* from the people who are just trying to *protect you*. But what you're starting to realize is that no matter how mad you get—or how much you are sure you don't want someone who brings you to this place and leaves you here—love doesn't go away just because a title does, does it?

And so that's when the questions really come. The ones you suddenly start to feel are *your* questions now. The ones you *can't* talk about with the people you normally talk about things with. The questions like—what if this was your fault? What if you made a big deal about something that wasn't even an issue? What if—*they* were really struggling with something and couldn't find the words to tell you about it? What if *you* pushed too hard or said the wrong things or weren't good enough or worse—what if you didn't give them a real chance? The benefit of the doubt? Patience? Unconditional love? *Time?*

So, following all of—*that*—you arrive at the most dangerous place you've been so far in your healing process. The place where you think—well, you don't have the answers. And the people who love you don't have the answers. And so the only answer is—*to call them*. To call them and get the answers that only *they* have. About your life. About how you got here. About whether this was the right choice. About whether they miss you. About—well, anything and everything that is *not* a part of the story you're currently telling but still wanting. Things that—if you were thinking with your head right now instead of your heart—you'd also realize they'd *had* a chance to tell you. You know? Back there in that place where it all went down? When you guys *ended* a relationship rather than choosing to work through it?

I say it like that because I *want* it to stick out to you. Look—I know you *may not* have had a say in how it happened. Or *that* it happened. I also know you may have had *years* to ask these questions and reflect on the answers you got or didn't get. But it doesn't matter. We all analyze and second-guess and look back. We do.

So, I know what you're thinking. You are thinking that—they *must* be sitting by the phone wondering if you're going to call to make it right. That—maybe this is an opportunity for you to change the way things happen from here. That—something *terrible* must have happened to them to make them do what they did. That—this *must* be all your fault and *you* are the only one with the power to make things right. Oh. And that *you* were way too hard on *them*.

Right?

Well.

Only you can decide how your love story gets written. Only you can decide whether you pick up that phone and open up that whole box again. And, because this is a decision that only you can make, I want to ask you a few questions. Three, actually. And I hope that you think long and hard about the answers before you dial those numbers. Or send that text. Or—yes—write that nice long *relationship overview* email you've been thinking so long and hard about. (Yes, I know about that.)

So here goes, love. Three questions.

One. You do realize that a phone can be dialed from both sides, right? Obviously you do. But what I mean is, *they* could call you, too. If they wanted to. They could reach back out and say I'm sorry. That they got it wrong. That they miss you. That they *want* to work things out. Want to change. Help. Heck—that they went temporarily insane. I mean, *whatever* reason they could give you would be infinitely better than the one they're giving you right now. And I know this is hard to hear, but *silence* is an answer. A loud one. And you reaching out opens you back up to the potential of getting hurt *even more*. It gives them the power to control the situation. It gives you the potential to call—or text—and get *more* silence in return. And that may hurt even more than where you are right now. Again—this is a decision only you can make. And I'm not telling you to be stubborn—I'm just telling you to think it through. Carefully. Because things *did* end (I know, there it is again) for a reason. Whether it was your reason. Or theirs. Or a little bit of both of yours. And honestly—are you *ready* right now for what happens if things don't go the way you're expecting? What if they don't answer? Don't call back? Answer and tell you something you aren't ready to hear? Just think about it, love. Because you're well into your healing right now—even in these little moments— and calling them is going to make you have to start all over again. Do you want that?

Two. This is a harder question, but I want you to really think through it anyway. I know you're doing everything to *forget* what happened. But for this moment, I want you to go back and remember how *you* felt when they said—or did—whatever they said or did. I want you to remember the way *their face looked*. Or how their absence felt. Or their silence. I want you to remember what those words made you feel. When they said them. Or didn't. I want you to focus on those hours—days—weeks— after the end came. In whatever way it did. And then, I want you to remember how broken you were. How confused. How insecure. How *alone*. And I want you to ask yourself—*could you ever be with them again and not think of how that felt?* Or, *could you ever* trust them with your heart again, completely, after all of this? Or—do you *really still think* one more chance is going to *fix* what broke you guys? Honestly. In what world could you go back and love them in the same way?

Think about it, love. Because sure, there *are* things that grow from these kinds of experiences. Sometimes, really good things. But that depends entirely upon the circumstances that got you and that other person to this moment. And love? Try to think about the answers to these questions without the *missing them* part driving the answer. Because I know when you're missing someone and trying to fill that empty space that is everywhere now—your answer is *always* going to be yes. It's going to be *yes*—I can trust them again. Yes—they can change. Yes—we can make this work.

And in certain circumstances, that may very well be the case.

Sometimes people *can* change. But the more likely outcome is that they won't.

And I know you already know this, but I'm going to say it anyway—you cannot *go back* to where you were *before* things ended. Things are *not* going to be the same. Oh, I know your head is telling you that you can pretty much rewind to that exact place you last left things. I know you think time has stood still in that space, leaving a chance for you to go back and fill it.

But it hasn't.

I know this is hard to hear, but—silence is an answer.
The loudest one you will ever hear.

Time *never* stands still. It is always moving forward—always changing— always shifting and moving as new circumstances are stirred into it by choice or chance or just plain old growth. And the truth is, you and that person you're missing are both completely different people now.

Standing in a different world. Sharing a new truth.

Three. This is the important question—but the hardest. The one you definitely *will not* have an easy answer for. But I think—when I ask you, you'll at least have some sort of immediate *gut* reaction. So, here it is. *What if it happens again?* I mean—what if you have to go through what you went through (*are* going through) *again?* Because that's entirely possible if you go back to what hurt you. You know this—you just may not want to admit it. Or face it. Or change as a result of it. But *you know*— like the old bumper-sticker version of love and loss says—when someone hurts you the first time, it's their fault. When they hurt you the second time, it's yours.

Now—to be clear, I *know* there are a million circumstances that make us stay with people who aren't good to us. Or *for* us. Some of those reasons are very difficult, very complex, very sensitive issues. You have your reasons, and I'm not negating or downplaying them in any way. **All I'm saying is—once you learn something about someone you didn't know—you arm yourself with the power to change how the future with them looks.** You cannot *unknow* what you know. So—I'll ask one more time. *What if it happens again?* Are you ok with that? Because this time, you'll be *even further* down the road. More time will have passed. And I promise you, you're either going to be much deeper in love—or infinitely more hurt and frustrated. Time is an amplifier—and it's going to *magnify* whatever it can in the process. So—while you're thinking through your answer to this one, I'm going to leave you with an oldie but goodie.

When people show you who they are, it's probably best that you listen.

**

So now that you have answers to those three questions—or at least, some idea how you feel—I want to explain just a little more to you about the art of breaking up. Look, I *get* that ending a relationship is not something any of us *want* to be good at. At the core, it means we have to hurt someone who loves us. And that is just plain old hard. But—it also means that we have to affect at least two—and in reality, *so* many more—lives in the process. Because being with someone gets you all tangled up in their world, doesn't it? With their families. Their friends. Their habits. Their homes. Their—everything.

And this is just one of those great truths about love. Because whether or not any of us *want* to be good at ending a relationship, *how* someone *does* an ending says *a lot* about them. And you want to know why? Because *the people who love us the most have the power to hurt us the most.* And the person who is driving an ending—is armed with it *all.* Our insecurities. Our vulnerabilities. Why we've had trouble trusting. Our bad habits. Our secrets. *Every little thing* we struggle with but hide from the rest of the world.

They have *all* the weapons to use in the end.

And that is why—when we do get there—what each of us *does* with the information we have collected is *what defines us.* It's a character thing. The objective is not to hurt someone who is already hurting. It's not to be right. It's not to get ahead. It's not to go back and assign blame. And it is *most certainly* not to dig up things from the past and fling them carelessly at each other like this is some sort of war someone wins. No one wins.

No one wins at the end of a love story. The story just—ends—and then, you each keep on writing your own.

The objective—if that is the place you both are in—is just to end it. With the least hurt possible. If someone knows you've been really hurt in your past—they aren't going to blow up a relationship with anger and coldness. They aren't going to hold back information you might need during your healing. They aren't going to throw things back in your face or withdraw into complete silence. Good people—*people with character*—are going to sit down with you and tell you—this isn't working for me anymore. I've changed. I need different things. I wish you all the best, but it needs to be over. They are *not* going to try to hurt you even more in the process of letting you go. They are not going to cheat on you and blame you for not giving them what they needed. They are not going to try to sabotage your life or your job or your other relationships in any way. Because, truthfully— if it's already over, there isn't really much more they need to say, is there?

**

We all go *in* to love knowing we can get totally hurt in the process. And that is why so many of us drag our feet early on—trying to predict whether *this* person and *that* situation are actually worth it. We all go in knowing how much it can hurt in the end—but, I think most of us can agree, no matter how we get there, that we never go in wanting to hurt someone we used to love. Someone who loved *us*.

And that's what I mean when I say how a breakup happens says a lot about someone.

Sure, you have to consider there is emotion and frustration—and maybe exhaustion or bad timing involved. You have to consider that sometimes, one person will push for answers that someone else isn't ready to give. Which means—sometimes the words *won't come out right*. But character doesn't take preparation, even if the words are messy. Character says, "I don't want this person to hurt any more than they have to." Character says, "I am going to be as clear as I can about what went wrong, so they don't overthink it too much later." Character says, "I used to love this person—or in some ways, I always will—so I'm going to be as honest as I can with them even though it's going to hurt us both." Character is what you want. It's what you want to date. And marry. And be.

If you find yourself looking at a stranger in the end—something is wrong there. If someone completely stops talking to you, or uses everything you gave them *against you*—something is wrong there. If you spend years building a relationship and it takes seconds to break it down—something is wrong there. And love? If they told you to trust them, and in the end—they don't even believe you deserve to understand, in the best way they can find words to tell you, *what went wrong*—something is wrong there. And I'm *really* going to encourage you to use those things as crucial signs that—*that*—was not your person. Trust me. It does get complicated. We do say things we don't mean. We say things we could have said better. Clearer. *Kinder.*

But, even if the love has faded, there should *always* be some part of that person you loved left that wants to protect you from pain.

Not to become the cause of it.

I need you to read that until you understand it.

And until you do—don't you dare pick up that phone.

**

6. "Throw *Out* the Toothbrush."

Throwing out the past so you can face the future.

O ne of my good friends and I just chatted on FaceTime tonight. She's also in the midst of navigating a difficult breakup. One that—after about a year and a half—ended because of some of those fundamental "core" differences. The *hard* kind. The ones where you *totally love* the person, but you *just know* they don't have what you need from (or in) a partner in the *lifetime* kind of way. I'm not going to tell her story—because it's hers. I will share, however, the progress she laughed about tonight as we talked about how to start this chapter.

"I finally threw out the toothbrush," she said.

"The toothbrush?" I inquired, smiling.

"Yeah," she continued, "I threw out the *evidence* that just keeps reminding me he's not here anymore. I threw it out because those little reminders— that derail me daily—are *not* helping this whole healing process. At. All."

A wise friend I have.

Anyway, we laughed about how many *toothbrushes* there are in the aftermath of a relationship. You know them—the things that remind you every single day that *they* used to be there, but aren't there, and are probably not coming back? *Those* are your toothbrushes. The kind, affectionate little name we can use to label the land mines. The *things* that jump out at us. That cause us to spin in a circle of—*I can't get rid of it*. Because it's theirs. And—they might be coming back. And—they might need it one day. And—*no*. Just stop there.

Guys. Your ex does *not* need the little things they left behind at your house. Generally. Unless they are some super personal, super expensive, three-hundred-year-old family heirlooms—throw them into a box and get them the heck out of your house. I mean it. They are just *things*. And while *things* definitely don't define what you had—they *will* remind you of it. Constantly. And that is *not* what you need.

Now. I also realize that some of you are reading that going *I lived with this person. My toothbrushes are my whole house.*

I get it. But the same logic still applies.

The point here is that *you need to sift through your life*. So, if you lived together, find all the things you *can never* rebrand as your own. The things that are inherently *theirs*. The things that make your stomach sink when you look at them. The things that have *memories* ground right into the very fibers of their being. And then do it. *Take some action.*

They are just *things.*
And while *things* definitely don't define what you had—
they certainly *will* remind you of it.

What does that look like? Maybe—give away the couch. Paint the room. Take down that picture that stares at you from the hallway. Move absolutely everything around. Or—even better, move all those trigger points into one room and shut the door. Shut it. And don't open it again until *you are ready*. You guys will work through *things* later. But for now, you don't need them visually harassing you every single time you see them. It's ok. No—really it is. This little *get it out of my sight* activity has nothing to do with you giving up on the potential that maybe one day you guys will work things out (I know you're still thinking that). It has *only* to do with the decision that for right now, the past is the past. And it's over. And you need to heal.

So do it.

Your *toothbrush* might look like a lot of things. A missing text message on your phone in the morning. The trip you planned together that is still on the part of your calendar you can't make yourself look at. A Wednesday night *without them* while you watch the next episode of the series you both loved. It might look like the fact that you now have to pour only one cup of coffee in the morning instead of two. Or, that you are your *own* workout partner. Or maybe it's their old tee shirt—the one you just can't bring yourself to wash because it still *smells* like them.

Your *toothbrushes* are what you have to deal with now. So let's work through that.

**

The hardest part about adjusting to your new life is figuring out what your new life *actually looks like*. And that's not going to be an easy puzzle to put together. Actually, on most days in the beginning, it's going to be like you are navigating your world for the first time. You won't be, of course, because the world is actually *exactly* the same as it always was. It's just that—as you know full well now—you're now having to do it *without* someone that used to do it with you. And that's hard.

So let me give you some little GPS coordinates that will help frame where you are right now.

One. Things you expect (and won't expect) are going to completely blindside you. Be prepared to be surprised.

Two. You're going to feel lonely—and alone—even when a bunch of people are around you. That's normal.

Three. *It is going to take time.* And no, no matter what you learn *about why*—you *cannot* fast-forward this part.

Those three things are like hall passes. Or *get out of jail free* cards to keep you out of trouble. And I promise, they will help you to navigate. So— for now, just read them. And store them away. Earmark this page, maybe. Because, when you *do* get all wrapped up in your toothbrush moments, those things will help you understand that you are exactly where you should be. And that this is all just a part of the process. And that some- times—going through all this means you're going to be taking *one* step forward and *two* steps back for a little while. It means you're going to smile and throw out the toothbrush in the morning. And collapse into a heap of tears by the evening.

That's ok, love. It won't always feel like this.

**

You'll find that one of the hardest things—which I guess makes sense, but you won't be prepared for—is while you're figuring *out* your new life, you're still going to be completely focused *on theirs.* You'll be sitting there—obsessing—about whether they are missing you. Whether they are dating. Whether this is hard for them too. Whether they are going out with their friends. What their friends are saying. Whether they *told* their friends. Whether they told their family. What their family said. Your mind will be going to them—again—over and over and over. When you need *all of it* to be focused on you.

Pull it back, love. This is *not* about them anymore.

Let me say it again. This is *not about them anymore.*

It's not about what they are doing. Or saying. Or their needs. Or reasons. Or issues. Or wishes. Or frankly, their—anything. Because from the moment things ended—they *lost* the chance to claim that much of your mental space. That's your real estate now.

And trust me, like I said, you need all of it.

**

I remember when I was navigating this phase in a former relationship—a much longer one—my *toothbrush* was the entire city of Chicago. We'd been together for over four years and that is where he was originally from. He loved the Chicago Cubs—had even bought me a jersey—and we'd spent some great times there with his family. Well, after we broke up it used to *physically hurt* anytime I heard anything about that city. Or saw the word. Or saw pictures of it. Or heard anything about *that* team. Or stadium. Or—I know—the things we do to ourselves. (P.S. Sorry if you're from Chicago. I've overcome this. I like the Bean. Promise.)

Now—to make matters worse, a short time after this intense disgust for all things Chicago erupted, I was booked on a flight that ended up connecting there. *For hours.* And I remember the panic that initially set in. And that feeling when I stepped off the plane and into that airport that was—his. Or—his and mine. It *literally made my stomach sink.*

And that experience was the first time I taught myself the lesson I am going to teach you. Four words popped into my head. Out of nowhere. In the midst of that spinning that he was *still* causing in my life. Months later. Four words: *Chicago. Is. Not. Yours.*

I wrote them down.

And then I spent every single one of those hours waiting for my next flight *rebranding* what my eyes were looking at. This was *not* his airport. This was not *our* airport. This was—*an*—airport. An airport where hundreds of thousands or perhaps millions of people set eyes on each other for the first time. Said goodbye for the last time. Hugged each other after a long time. Met. Fell in love. Broke up. Got bad news. Got amazing news. Or—just simply walked through on their way to somewhere else.

All of your places are like that too. And right now, I know that's hard to see because your eyes are still so caught up in the view of you and that person you're missing so hard. But your things will be your things again. Teach your eyes to look at them the way they are—not the way they were.

Because, *that* is where progress comes from.

**

Ok. So one last thing. And I do think we need to address this one directly. Because while we do each have *our own* unique little toothbrushes, *most of us* have at least one that is fundamentally, completely, 100% the same. And it's a big one. And with this one, most of us—the same people who are reading a whole book about healing—are going to outright *torture* ourselves. Willingly. Knowingly. Repeatedly.

Guys. I'm talking about social media.

I don't care *how much* you think you want to know what they are up to. I don't care whether they are a *great* person. I don't care whether you think one day you can *totally* be friends. Or you're trying to be right now. I don't care whether you have kids with this person or you *need* to know what they are up to because without that information, your brain will drive you completely crazy.

Block them. Unfriend them. Unfollow them.

I mean it. And don't worry about how they are going to perceive it. This isn't about being mean. It's not about trying to hurt them. It's not about *proving* a point. Or *making* a point. Or making it *look* like you're over them. This is only about you. And what is best for you. If you're still talking, or you need to be for whatever reason—then just tell them that. Say—look, I need to do this for me. And then make sure you tell yourself now that *it doesn't matter whether they understand.* Whether it makes them mad. Whether it affects how they feel about you. You are not asking for their permission *or* their opinion. Do you hear me? Part of your healing is figuring out how *not* to continue rubbing an open wound. Because that's what *seeing them* every day on some social media platform when they *aren't yours anymore* is. An open wound.

Stop the bleeding. Let it heal. Let *yourself* heal.

Stalking their social media to look at *what* pictures they are posting or *who* they are with or *where* they are or *what time of day* they are online or *who* is commenting or how *often*—is just not healthy for you. Ever. I don't care how much your head tells you it is—I don't care how much you think you need to know that stuff. Or see it.

Take that toothbrush out of your life completely.

And do it immediately.

Oh, and love? I want you to keep them out *of your social media feed* for long enough that the active hurt actually fades. For long enough that *every single thought* doesn't go directly to them. For long enough that you *stop caring about* what *could* show up in their social media feed. You'll know when it's time. But I'll tell you, it should be a place where your first thought every morning isn't how much it hurts. Where you *forget* a little. Or a lot. That is how you'll know you are healing. And I think, what you'll find, is that after you've forced yourself to do this little—let's call it a *cleanse*—you're going to be *really comfortable* keeping it that way.

Trust me. You just have to get past this initial part where it seems like the last thing you could ever do. So here's the challenge. Do it for, let's say—ninety days. Just ninety days. Promise me—promise yourself—that you will do that. Even when the curiosity is *killing you.* Even if someone tells you something about what they are up to. Even if they start dating again. Even if they reach out to you. Hold strong. And when you get to the end of that ninety days, ask yourself that hard question we already talked about. The one about healing. The one that goes something like: now that it's been so long—and you've made so much progress in all this—do you *really* want to go back and get all wrapped up in that spinning again?

Chances are, the answer will be no.

**

When we let someone love us—we give them a space within us. In our hearts. In our lives. And the longer they stay with us, the larger that space becomes. It keeps growing and growing—pushing up against all the other spaces we have kept saved within us—for family. For best friends. For our wildest, craziest dreams. For our pasts. Our regrets. Our one. And sometimes, that space we give them grows so big that it spills over and gets all tangled up with everything else.

And that is why—that simple fact—is why it's *so hard* to let people go.

When they rip themselves out of that place we had saved and protected for just them—not only do we have to untangle all those other pieces, but we also have to figure out how we go about *filling* that big hole that their absence has left behind. And it's scary. Seeing how empty that place is where someone used to be. I know it hurts. I know life feels empty when there are entire parts of you needing to be filled. But I also know that—even more fundamentally true than how much you're hurting right now is that *you want someone who stays.* You want someone who takes that space you give them and builds something. For you. Within you. With you.

Let me say that again. *With you.*

**

Ok. So, let's tie up the toothbrush chapter. And actually, just to round this out—I want to give you one other way you could think about this. If the toothbrush analogy didn't work for you—think of the "used to" things and "way things were" moments like land mines. Yes, land mines. Land mines that are buried absolutely everywhere in all the places you're used to walking in your life. That you *have* to walk. And, while you're going about your new life—struggling already—they *come out of nowhere*. They completely derail you. They tilt you off your axis.

They bring you back to the depths of that *they aren't here anymore* and *things aren't the same* spinning. And just for the record, I also want you to know that it won't always be the big things you're expecting that will get you the most. The small things are what you need to prepare yourself for. And—no matter what, again—just know there isn't a trick to this. The only thing you have to do now is keep walking. *That* is your objective. Keep moving. And what will happen, slowly, is you'll go about finding those land mines—before you step on them. And then you'll dig them up carefully. Disarm them. And put them in a place that makes your world safe for you to walk around in again. But trust me when I say that you can't do that if you avoid everywhere you know they are buried. You can't do that if you refuse to face those places and things you know are going to hurt.

So, like my friend told me tonight—*throw away the toothbrush*. Do it.

But—
you want someone **who stays.**

And then, slowly, a little bit every single day, take those things back that have an "us" label. And make them *yours* again. Go to the restaurant. Watch the show. Make the coffee. Wash the sheets. Throw away the rose you dried from that first bouquet they gave you. Take down the pictures. Erase the birthday reminder from the calendar. Delete the text message history.

Untangle, love.

Untangle.

**

7. "I Keep *Forgetting* I Can't Call."

Wanting to talk to someone who isn't yours.

This is the chapter that changes every time. And the reason it does, is because *this* is where you get to the *personal* part of the healing process. The place where you are forced to deal with the *real* things the person you loved brought to your life. The moments. The memories. The laughter. The inside jokes. The things *only* the two of you would ever really understand.

The things that *built* your love story.

And that is why this part will hit you so hard. Because as you feel your way through it—there will be so many times that you catch yourself forgetting that things *aren't* the same. And you will go to pick up the phone. To call them. To text them. *To tell them.* And you'll be forced to feel the sting of the truth like it's the first time all over again.

So—this is the *missing them* chapter.

The one where you figure out—*often*—how hard it is to *untangle* your life from theirs. And like so many things in this process, *what* you will find yourself missing *most* is not going to be what you expect. You have a list—you've always had a list—of the things you loved about them. And I'll bet—like, I'll really bet—that *those* are not going to be the things that you think about. What's going to happen is you're going to miss things you didn't even know *were things*. Things you didn't even notice at the time. That you didn't think were an essential part of who they were. And what you'll find is *those things* are going to be beautiful, complicated little reminders of what was an undeniably unique characteristic of that person you loved. And I'm sorry to put this out there just like that, but—*these things* are going to hit you hard. Really hard.

Maybe what you'll notice *after* it all goes down is *your person* had this little pause right before they laughed. Maybe you'll find that it was the way they slightly mispronounced a word. Or the completely out-of-order way they used to do something that everyone else has an order for. Maybe it will be hearing one of those *ten-dollar words* that only they used to use. Or the way their smile tilted a little more on the right side than the left. Maybe it's going to be the way their eyes sparkled when they saw you. Or how every single time you rode the elevator, you had to kiss before you got to your floor. Maybe it was the way they always grabbed first for your hand. Or how they liked their coffee. Or how easy it was to tell them how hard your day was. Maybe it was the way they held you like you were *the best and only thing* in their world. Or—maybe it's simply the echo of them saying—*we're in this together*.

So, yes—you're going to have your list. You won't know exactly what it's going to look like—but trust me when I say that your list is going to write itself pretty quickly. And as it gets longer, I want you to remember something for me. About healing. About love. About memories. I want you to remember that *every single thing* you put on that list was something that *built* a love story that meant something to you. Something real. Those were your—building blocks. And just as you discovered each one of those things slowly—over time—it's also going to take *time* for those things to come off of that list, too. To fade into the blur of regular memories of someone and something that no longer hurts.

Do you understand that? It takes *time* to work through all of the hard stuff that got you here.

Just like it's going to take time to stop missing the good stuff that held you *there*.

**

You know, it's going to surprise you. How this part works. And I wish I could tell you I have the roadmap. The one that will help you navigate this—lessen the pain. But unfortunately, I don't. *I can't.* And I don't because—while I can tell you *so many things* about how it will feel and what you can do to make it *easier*—the truth is, *this* part isn't about anyone except you. And *what you had with them.*

In the last chapter, we talked a lot about toothbrushes. The things in a relationship we *have* to let go of because of how they hold us back. *This* chapter is going to deal with a similar set of circumstances, but, in some ways—is going to be completely different. Because, this chapter isn't about things and places. It's about *them*. It's about the things you can't just rebrand. Or throw out. Or stop missing. These aren't the things in your life you can identify and work through externally. These are the things you're going to need to work from the inside out. And this chapter—it is an important one. So—let's start with a nice little laundry list of things that are probably going to set you off.

Just so you're prepared.

Your stomach is probably going to flip when a car that looks like theirs drives by. Or when you meet someone that has the same name. You're going to miss like crazy all those little things you would have texted or emailed each other. Or worse—when something reminds you of the *inside jokes* only the two of you understood. Then there will be the anniversaries. Sad songs. Good songs. Their songs. Your song. *Any song.* And the simple, beautiful way you were when you were with them—and they were with you. The nicknames. The calls. The laughter about the things no one else would even think was funny. Your favorite meals. Snacks. Movie nights. Road trips. Those darn Facebook memories that pop up out of nowhere. The entire text message thread you can't bring yourself to delete. How you used to sink into the couch with them at the end of a long hard day. Or week. When something happens only they would appreciate. The countless times you find yourself picking up the phone to tell them—and remembering they aren't *yours* anymore. Learning to do things *alone.* Listening to other people tell stories about them that you didn't know first. Their smell. Their voice. The touch of their hand. How they brushed the hair from your forehead gently. *The way they looked at you.*

But mostly—how *quickly* all those things you loved became the things that hurt.

**

It takes *time* to work through
the hard stuff that got you here—
just like it's going to take time
to stop missing the good stuff
that held you *there*.

I got the idea for this chapter while I was getting ready for work this morning. I'm telling you—when you're a writer and navigating a breakup—the world is one entire writing prompt. It's definitely one of those times you need *something* to write on *everywhere*.

Anyway.

I put my favorite morning show on the iPad and was listening to people call in and talk about all the things they were doing. This guy called in and said like three words—I don't even remember what they were—but *something* about the tone or the emphasis or the way it sounded like he smiled when he talked—floored me. It launched me into the spin. Of thinking about the person who has somehow prompted such a short little complicated chapter of my life that it compelled me to write an entire book.

Let me say that more eloquently.

I was triggered by *the voice* of someone *I don't know* talking about something *I don't remember* on a radio station *I'm not even listening to anymore*. And I'm not listening to it because—instead—I'm writing this chapter. In this book. About missing them.

So let's do this. Let's break it down. Let's really get to the heart of how *and why* those small little things you didn't even know were part of someone can completely change how you look at your world.

**

Let's just start with the most basic of truths. How you feel. Because one thing I think most of us *get really confused* about when we end a relationship is that. How *should* we feel now? I mean, we certainly feel a lot of things in those first couple hours and days and weeks. I get it. But that's not what I mean—that emotional part that comes first. What I mean is—on one hand, we've removed a title. Whether it was girlfriend or boyfriend or fiancé or husband or wife or partner or—some other little adorable nickname you guys had—**what we learn quickly is that removing a title *does not* remove the feelings that built it.**

Let me be clearer.

There was love there. I mean, you stayed with this person because you saw something (or a lot of somethings) in them. You gave this person the most incredible piece of your life that you can. *Your time.* You guys *chose* each other for an entire chapter of this life. And that means that *at least part* of that memory has *got* to be worth saving, right?

So, to get through this, I'm going to encourage you to think about this experience in two neat little boxes. Maybe that will help you make sense of how the past and the present can fit together now. In one box, put the person you loved—the one you miss. The one you made all those incredible memories with. In the other, I want you to put the person you *know now.* The one that let the pain and complicated feelings and confusion into your world.

And then I want you to keep those two boxes completely separate. At least for now.

What I mean is—while I would never encourage you to miss the first person and ignore the truth of the second—what I *will* encourage you to do is give yourself permission to let that first person *keep* the part of you they built. Does that make sense? Just because a relationship ended doesn't mean you have to go back in time and rebrand everything they said and did with the same eyes you see them with now. Just because the ending was messy doesn't mean the beginning and the middle weren't worth it.

Stories change. They develop in ways we could never have expected. And the truth is, maybe we don't *ever* really unlove people—and maybe that's exactly how it's supposed to be. We just learn to let the people we've loved keep that part of us they made, and then we keep going and find someone who will one day love us more. In a different way. And you know, maybe that's also the beauty of time. And endings. And healing. Because our heart builds on what it knew first—but it builds something bigger. More powerful. Your heart will never completely let you forget anything that once made it happy.

So I want you, during this *missing them* chapter, to let yourself keep the part of you that loved them. It's as simple as that. And that is *not* unhealthy. Don't throw out any part of your heart that spent its time learning how to love.

Because that is never a bad lesson.

No matter who (or what) got to teach it.

**

I think you just need to accept this one, love. Endings are just plain old confusing. And abrupt. And *hard*. I know I'm not telling you something you don't already know. But I feel compelled to say it anyway. Just to make sure it's part of how you're processing this.

Endings don't come with the answers we want—and even if they did— we probably wouldn't understand them much at the time because of that whole *we're listening with our hearts* thing that we do when there are emotions involved. So, because endings are confusing (whether you've been working through things or they come out of nowhere)—*how* and *when* a relationship ends is always going to surprise you. No matter how you get there, you arrive at that moment when you are watching someone you love walk away. You arrive at that moment when there is, maybe, one last hug. One last look. One last door closing behind them.

And you know what's hard about that?

Everything. Everything is hard about that.

Because, other than death, there are very few things in this life that we have to let go of in that way. So—completely. So—fundamentally. So—painfully. Where feelings and memories and pasts and histories and lives are all tangled up in each other. And it just—*stops*—one day.

I used to think it was ironic that we lived in a world that wants insurance for just about everything. But when it comes to the one thing that *truly* has the greatest power to affect us—we get absolutely no guarantees. No promises. No forevers. Just—blind trust. And faith. And hope.

So what I want you to understand about this first piece of the *missing them* chapter is that **it's ok to miss them.** And it's also ok to be scared of what comes next and what it's going to feel like. I know you *think* you never want to trust someone again. I know you *think* the answer is to go back through your relationship to see if you can see the signs. Just—don't. And don't because people are not projects. Or puzzles. Or problems to solve. And you can't go back and piece together a story—or analyze it—just because you know the ending. What I want you to do is just accept that endings create a—hole—in your life. And even if that hole is someone else's fault, *you* are now completely responsible for filling it. And love, you *will*.

**

So let's talk about that. Filling holes in your life. Because they are everywhere, aren't they? I know, like we talked about in the last couple of chapters, that you're really trying your best to figure out what life looks like right now. But what I need you to realize is that, when that relationship ended, a *whole lot more* than just a person left your life. You lost your daily routine. Your plans for the weekend. The plus-one events. You lost your shared little secrets. And their friends. And families. And, yes—*you* lost *your* friend, too, didn't you? Because, first and foremost, that's probably what they were, right? Your friend. So all these places that used to be filled with *them* are now glaring holes in the space you're navigating. And just like the *toothbrushes,* you have to figure out how to fill the holes they left in your life. And unfortunately, no one else can do that for you. And—I hate to say this, but this is definitely another one of those areas where there is simply no trick.

The best advice I can give you is just to *take it one step at a time*.

I know. I wish I could give you more. But I'll tell you—the absolute best and most effective thing you can do right now is just get to work.

One hole at a time. Whatever comes first.

**

So what do you need to remember in this part? That's simple. You need to remember that it is *ok* to miss them. It is *ok* to miss the person you spent a part of your life loving. Please don't put this whole thing in the *bad experience* bucket. There were a lot of things you got out of this. And *so many more* that you will. I'm not sure any type of ending is actually easy—but there are definitely some that are *way harder* than others. Topping that list? The ones where you have way more questions than answers and you're supposed to heal your own heart when you can't even understand what broke it. Someone told me yesterday that not everything has a lesson for us. Some things just fall in the category of really awful experiences that don't have good explanations. Those things, they said—are much, *much* harder to heal from. Because *we* are the ones standing alone at the end, left with the full responsibility of untangling all the knots someone else tied into us.

But you *can* untangle the knots.

And you *will* grow from this experience of loving them.

Even if they walked away holding what you think right now is your entire heart—you *will* figure out how to do life again. And trust me when I say: you will *be better* for having gone through this.

Even if for now, it has to hurt.

**

And the truth is—
**maybe we don't ever
really *unlove* people.**
We just learn to let them
keep the part of us they made,
and keep going until we
find someone who will
one day love us
more.

8. "*One* Step Forward, *Two* Steps Back."

The seesaw of weakness and strength.

There's something else you need to learn about untangling. Actually, as you're probably discovering *quite* well right now—there's a lot you needed to learn. That you *still* need to learn. That—actually— you never *wanted* to learn. And I know, some of it comes easier than others. Some of it comes more quickly than others. But this part—this part might be something you'll have to write down somewhere that you'll see it constantly.

Because I promise that you'll forget.

You'll need to write this down somewhere it can constantly remind you of how progress works. How—healing—works. And I'm sure you know this, but—none of it happens in a straight line. I know in concept that will make sense to you. But when it hits you, and it will—you'll lose all that rational thought you think you have now, and you'll beat yourself up. For—calling. For—texting. For asking for the millionth time *if they were sure this is what they wanted.* For going back. For having doubts. For—being weak.

Yes. It's ok. Weak is something we consider a bad word—but it's also just the opposite of strength. Which means, *sometimes* we *are* going to feel weak. And so that's why I need you to understand—*well*—how the cycle of healing works. Because you will feel strong one hour—one day. And weak the next. And then you'll decide you don't like how weak feels, so you'll pick yourself up. And do whatever you need to do to feel better. And your strength will return. And it will stay until—something—tips you off balance again.

And that's the seesaw. The back-and-forth journey we're all on until we get ourselves completely balanced again. And that's the place where we can *get off* the ride.

And so *that* is what we need to explore next. The seesaw. Of how. And *why.*

For me, it happens in the quiet moments. I told you how I feel about the mornings. How it all seems to hit at once, there in that morning sunlight. But—that also goes for the weekends, too. Your feelings of weakness are likely going to come in those moments when life slows down a little. The moments you very rarely give to someone else unless *they* are the someone else that *you* chose to let into your world. That makes sense, right? It's in the quiet moments when you are alone with your heart and mind. Alone with—your memories of them. Your insecurities about why this all happened. Your fears about what it means for your future.

All those *things* that can keep you focused and busy—that can make you avoid what *this* all actually feels like—those are just the façade, love. That you're over it. That this didn't affect you. That you're *good* with it. That it makes sense. But you cannot run from what you need to deal with—it's always faster than you. And it eventually will catch up.

Is it catching up?

Look, everyone approaches this part differently. Some of us face it head-on. And want to. But others—others avoid it for as long as possible. So we *don't* have to feel it. And in some cases, maybe that's for the best, at least in the beginning. It's how we protect ourselves from feeling things that are too hard for us to comprehend. But what happens, is when we avoid healing (or feeling) for too long, *all those things* we're trying to bury in places they can't stay—start bubbling up to the surface. Naturally. Unexpectedly. Forcing us to deal with the things we weren't ready to deal with.

And so that's where you decide how long you want to ride the seesaw.

Because you know, the way I see it—those things that bubble up are not signs any of us are stepping backward in our progress. They are *sure* signs that we're moving forward. Because the *only* way we can ever untangle the knots we have, love, is when we can see them. And feel them. And not be fearful of what they look like. Right up there in the open—near the surface—where people can see them.

**

So what does this part look like? And how is it really going to feel? Well— you will feel like you can *do* this. You will feel like you're *ok* not having all the answers because you have convinced your heart that you want someone who stays. Who communicates. Who doesn't cheat on you. Who loves your kids. Who is—*whatever.* In those times, you will think you don't need answers because you can keep yourself busy. And focus on yourself. And go to the gym. And reconnect with those friends you lost touch with a little. You'll reorganize your place. Buy some new clothes. Go out on the town. Throw yourself into work. And that will last—well, it *won't last* very long.

At least not continuously.

What happens is that phase lasts for just about as long as you can keep your eyes focused completely forward. With no distractions. No bumps in the road that cause you to look up and remember that you're doing this alone again. And those distractions—those *bumps* in the road—are inevitable. You can call them toothbrushes. Land mines. But whatever the case, what happens is those things jar you from your "I can do this phase," and make you *remember.*

What you miss. Where you are. Where you wanted to be.

And how *very far away* you are from being in that place.

And that's where the spinning starts. That strength you've been working so hard on crumbles completely. And you're back on the couch. Curled up in your bed. Not answering the phone. Not eating well. Skipping the gym. Saying no to your friends. You're—sad. You feel alone. And lonely. And—you feel like you might always be alone. And that feeling of loneliness is what triggers the next part of the spin. The overthinking. And that leads to the—*maybe they're missing me* part. So then you want to call. To fix this. And you arrive at that place where you're certain you want to go back. But you *can't* go back.

When you avoid *feeling* for too long,
all those things you're trying so hard to bury
just eventually start bubbling up to the surface.
You think it's a sign you're moving backward—
when it's actually a sign you're moving forward.
The only way you can untangle the knots, love,
is when you can see them. And feel them.

And—just slow down, love. Slow down. (And P.S., if you want to call, please refer to everything we just talked about in the *Don't You Dare Pick Up That Phone* chapter.)

So I think what you need right now is some anchor points. A few things you can latch onto safely, that will ground you. Maybe—that will even start to frame how you're going to feel walking through this, before we get to what *you* need to do with all of it. Here goes.

What you're feeling right now has a lot more to do with *you* than them. What I mean is—*sure* you're missing them. But what you're probably missing more is the life *you had* when you were with them. You're missing the routine. The secrets. The laughter. You're missing how much you liked your regular Wednesday nights and looked forward to your weekends. You're missing how much more interesting your trips to the grocery store were. How—even the little things didn't feel like little things when you guys were together. Right?

And, if you were *really* honest, maybe you could also see that what you're really missing—even more than all those things you loved about them— is the connection. The way you *had* someone and they had you in all those little moments the rest of the world doesn't get a chance to share with you. And that's the real part, love. When *anything* leaves our lives, we are forced to relearn how to do things we'd gotten really used to—and good at—doing another way. It's comfort. And we *thrive* on comfort.

So, as time ticks by in this whole untangling process, I want you to understand that one simple truth. How what you're feeling is probably *way less* about missing them than you think. Oh, I know you *do* miss them. But I also know that you're going to feel this way every single time you end something with someone. Maybe that's not what you want to hear right now. But you will. Because this isn't the part that's *personal* to them—it's the part that is *common* to all of us. At the core of who we are, we *all* just want to be loved. When love goes away, we feel vulnerable. And alone. And insecure. And it *always* feels confusing. We all deal with it differently, but we *all* feel it. This part where we have to make sense of a new place we've just walked into. And couldn't really prepare for.

So remember that, ok? Remember there are two separate parts of what you're feeling right now. One is certainly about them and what they brought to your life. But—the other isn't. The other is about you. And me. And—all of us. *The human part.* Oh. And one more thing? Just because I think you might need to hear it right now. That second part, where you're missing that connection? That's the *dangerous* part that makes you want to go back. And the part that convinces you it's *easier* to go back than to move forward. But love? You don't stay with someone just because you loved the life you had with them. That's not the glue that is going to fix these pieces.

Trust me.

**

You look at the world around you now and everyone has someone, don't they? The things you used to smile at now make your stomach turn. Oh, love. I get it. And that is why you need to hear the second anchor point. And let's just say it how it is:

It is *hard* to be alone.

There's no sugarcoating that. I'm not going to justify or explain it. It's just *hard.* And that's the other part of what you're feeling right now.

You've been forced into this crazy place where you don't know how to navigate anymore and that's bad enough. The being lost. But what's worse—is you *are* doing it alone. You thought, before this all went down, that you *finally* found that someone who filled the space in your heart that always seemed to be empty. You thought you had the *thing*. The *connection*. The *one*.

And so now? Now—you are starting to look in every pair of eyes you see for what you thought you had. Wondering whether any of them will *ever* see you the way you want to be seen. The way—*they*—saw you once. But—and I know this is a hard time to hear this—someone else cannot complete you. I know you know that. I know you *get* that. I know, reading that, it may even sound a little cliché. But I also know, when you're done being tough and self-assured and brave—that you can probably admit you spend your lifetime looking for it. That thing. That person with the magic. The answers. The connection that fills the part of you *nothing else* in this world has the power to do. The one that makes everything we go through to find them *worth* it.

And that is why this is such a hard truth.

On one hand, love *should* give us more than we had without it. But on the other—we have *got* to understand the difference between growing something new with someone else and *filling* something of our own. We're going to talk a lot about that in the last part of this book. But looking for someone else to give you what you need to fix yourself? Or fill yourself? *That* is where we usually break relationships. Because—we come in *not whole* and we expect someone else to glue us together. And, when they can't, we break a little more. So we need a little more glue. So we look more and more urgently for the next person holding the bottle.

And that's all I mean here. And I do have some ways to help you through this. We'll get to those. But for right now, I just want you to understand that you might have done that a little. Used them to fill those empty spaces you carry in your own heart. The ones you got from someone—or something—else. That you haven't dealt with yet. And that means that another *huge* part of your pain right now is *also not about them.* It's about you. And their absence is just making you feel that. Again. Right up there near the surface where you can't hide from it.

**

So what do you *do* from here?

Whether you've decided *everything* you're feeling is really about them— or you have started to consider that maybe what you're feeling is actually a mix of things, *that* is the real question right now, isn't it?

And I think the answer is pretty simple. And that's good. Because all the rest is too darn complicated, isn't it? So let's break it down. This—this part—is your comma. It might not be *quite* a period at the end of a sentence—or the word at the end of a book—but it *is* a pause. A place where you can *stop* and really evaluate who you are and what you want and what—*you*—want to do with that. It's where you can reflect on what you need from a relationship. And what you want for yourself. And who you are with other people. And what you are passionate about. And what—*you*—need to deal with in your life. For you.

Looking
for someone else
to give you what you need
to fix yourself—or fill yourself—
is where we break most relationships.
We come into love *not whole*, and then expect
someone else to know how to glue us together.
And when they can't, we just break a little more.
And then next time, need a lot *more glue.*

Because that's the real place we need to work on, love. Whether it's just about them or you're carrying a lot of things you haven't had a chance to put down yet. If you walked into that relationship with your hands all full of yesterday, then you didn't give it a chance. And if you choose, right now, to walk *into the next one* with your hands even more full, it has the potential to happen again. A high potential. If you don't deal with your pain—if you don't make it something you focus on and work through and face—it is going to *become a part of you.*

Do you get that?

If you don't face this—work through this—then your pain is going to become a permanent part of you that you *have* to carry with you. One that will make your hands so full that you can't hold theirs in the way you want to. Or that they need you to. And the longer you avoid what you're feeling, the more *power* you give your experiences to shape how all the stories from here will be told. Because what happens, is for every minute or hour or month or year that you don't deal with your pain—*more and more things in this life get piled on top of it.* And it gets pushed further and further down— into a place that's harder and harder to reach. And the harder that reach becomes? The easier it becomes to ignore it. Because it takes a lot of digging. And all that digging takes time. And energy. And yes, sometimes, pain.

But you *can't* ignore it forever.

So—did you hide what you were carrying, love? Long enough to fall in love? To make them fall in love with you? Because the thing about *baggage* or *scars* or whatever you want to label them—is that eventually you're not going to be the only one carrying them. You *think* they are yours, so you don't need to talk about them. Share them. Explore them. Especially with someone else that you want to think you're *great.*

And flawless. And—the one. But when you go into a relationship, there comes a point where, whether the other person wants to or not—they *have* to help you carry them. And—maybe they weren't ready for that. Or prepared. Or—maybe they found out, a little too late, that what you were carrying was just a little too heavy. Because maybe *their* hands were already full of what *they were carrying*.

And that's what I mean. When we really get to the heart of reflecting on what breaks the relationships we have and lose. When we get past all the surface-level reasons—the silence, the cheating, the communication (or whatever)—we get to the real *heart* (pun intended) of the issue. Whether either of us, or both of us, were actually *ready*. To be *in love*.

To be—*emotionally available.*

But so many times—*so* many times—what happens is that one or both of us weren't. And one or both of us didn't know. I mean, you *never* know in the beginning. I think that's what people mean when they say dating is the biggest lie. Or—that people have layers. And walls. And chapters they'll never read out loud. Because we all hide some of what we carry.

Maybe it's because we *can't* talk about it. Maybe it's that we don't know *how* to talk about it. Or worse—maybe it's because *we don't even know* that we're carrying it because we've pushed it so far down we can't even see it anymore. But whatever the case, those things we carry need to be held. In our hands. With us. As we walk through this life. And so when we meet someone and want to hold their hand, we have to figure out how we *look* like we're ready to do that. And so maybe we put all that stuff we're carrying down for a while. Or maybe we spend our time juggling all of it—so it looks like our hands are empty enough to hold theirs. But the trouble with that? It doesn't work forever.

And it doesn't work for *forward.*

Eventually, to walk into the future, you either have to unpack all that baggage, love, or you have to pick it up and carry it with you. And that is the place *so many people* individually make a choice that affects the *us.* If someone isn't ready to unpack what they are carrying, or they can't—then they *have* to carry all that with them while they are trying to hold a heart. And even if they are really strong, eventually, everybody gets tired. They get tired of trying to balance what they *want things to look like* with how they *actually are.* And that's where we face the hardest of all these truths.

Whether we, or they—were actually *ever* really all-in. Or even had the power to be.

**

So where does that put us? I know that's a lot of—*serious stuff.* If it's about them, you don't know any of the answers and that makes you feel worse. If it's about you—then maybe you're not ready to deal with all that. Or, maybe—just starting to realize that you even need to.

Either way, what I want you to remember is *progress,* especially when we're healing from relationships, is not linear. You heard me say that already. So—here's how that breaks down. You can't say, as much as you'd like to, that it's been *this long* so you should feel *that way.* I know, we all wish healing came with a *how-to* guide and a timeline. But that's where the one step forward, two steps back comes in. Because some days, some hours—some *whatever measure of time you're using*—you're going to have to go sideways, or even backward, to get what you need to move forward. And the objective *is* forward. So if that's what you need, or if that's what *happens,* go a little easy on yourself. I mean it. No one is judging your pieces—your drafts—your almosts. And the only thing that matters is that you *do* make progress. Eventually.

So focus on making it. I mean it.

What could you do—right now—that you could label as progress? As *one single step* forward in those *so many miles* you know you need to walk? There is something—there is *always* something you have the power to control. To start. To use. Something that could make you feel like you had a *little* more peace. A little more *balance.* A little more control in this chaos you're walking through. It doesn't need to be pretty—or completely thought through. It doesn't need to make sense or be something anyone else would understand. It just needs to be—*a step.* For you. That binds you to the next—and gets your feet moving. Maybe you start by admitting something out loud. Or deleting something that hurts. Maybe you ask for help. Give something up. Change your morning routine. Make that appointment. Whatever it is—just know, love, that big change always grows *from the single decision* that change is necessary.

And today is as good a day as any will ever be. You know that.

There's an old Chinese proverb I love—and it says, *the best time to plant a tree was twenty years ago. The second-best time is now.* I love it because that is *exactly* how growth works. I mean—we can always go back and wish we'd started sooner. But the point is, one day we actually *have* to take that first step. And do it. Because for anything (including us) to grow, we have to first plant the seed. And that is a step no one can (or will) do for us.

And then some days
you will *have* to go backward—
**to get what you need
to move forward.**

So do it. For you.

Oh—and one last thing. While you're working to get where you're going—just know it's ok to make some mistakes along the way. To feel weak. To go backward a little—or to go backward a lot. You *don't* always have to move forward to *be* moving forward. You don't have to win every single day.

Just in the end, love. *Just* in the end.

**

9. "I'm Going to Be Alone Forever."

The lies your heart tells you when it's broken.

So—now it is finally time to start doing what *you think* you aren't ready for. What you think, maybe, *you'll never* be ready for. But we're going to move in that direction anyway, ok? Because we need to start making the shift. Away from what *has happened*—and toward what *is happening.* Look—I know you don't have answers and you still want them. I know you *think* you haven't had enough *time* yet—and maybe you haven't. I'm sorry for that. But we need to do this. And we need to do it because unless you push yourself sometimes, you get stuck in a place where you can't totally move forward but you can't totally go back.

And I don't want you to get stuck.

Trust me—you will *never* feel ready to deal with the things you weren't ready for in this life. Does that make sense? I mean—it's all well and good when we can wait it out and analyze and plan—and then make our decisions when we have *just* the right amount of information and time to do it. But *more* than the majority of the time, you're just not going to get that. And you know it. And so, sometimes, you have to *force* yourself forward until the laws of science take over for you. Yes, I said it. *Science.* You know—objects in motion remain in motion? And objects at rest remain at rest? Nice little high school science lesson about inertia. But anyway—*that* is what you need. You need inertia. And to get it, you need energy. And to get energy, you *just* have to start moving. And then *keep* moving.

Yes, you will take two steps back for every step forward sometimes—and that will make you *feel* like you're ultimately moving backward. You're not. Because eventually, after you force yourself forward for long enough, you create a new normal. And that new normal and that new *energy* propel you. And the past loses its grip on you. And you start to heal.

And that is what *this* is about.

Not just all this sifting through the past and worrying about the future—but *progress.* I mean—at some point soon, for your health and happiness—you have *got* to decide how you want to close this chapter. And what you want to *learn* from it. But most importantly, you have to decide what part of this *you will take forward* as a permanent part of yourself.

Because you *will* get to decide.

And sure, this whole situation might not have been something you had any control over. I get it. But that's life too, isn't it? We rarely get to decide what happens to us. And maybe, in some crazy way, that's part of the beauty of it. What we *do* with what we *get*—especially when we never wanted it to begin with. And *that* is what the second part of this book is about. What you take away from this. And how that is going to shape you.

**When you force yourself forward—
you create a new *normal.***
And that *new normal* propels you.
And the past *loses its grip* on you.
And *that* is when you start to heal.

And I know you won't believe me right now, but what you take away from this whole experience *does not* have to be something negative. It *could* be something incredible—if you wanted it to be. Do you? But before we can get there, to that place we can start making decisions, we have to get past a few more things. And reflect on them. Because if we process these things right, what will come out of this *will* be something good. I mean it. I'm almost tempted to have you stop right now and write it down— how you feel. I want you to write down how many doubts you have. How many questions there are about *why* it had to happen. And yes, especially how little you believe that *anything* good could ever come from it.

I'm sitting here as the sun sets on a warm summer night in upstate New York, writing—and I'm smiling. (I'm visiting my family in the country.) I'm smiling because I know that if you *did* write down how you feel *right now*, and came back to it in a year or so—maybe even sooner—you would know the truth. About how *wise* time really is. About how it gives you just what you need when you need it, even though you fight it.

Thinking you know better. Thinking *you* have the answers.

Look—right now, you're living something that is going to shape your whole entire life. In a good way. And in a year, I promise that you will see it. And it will make perfect sense—*how many things were beginning* in all these moments it seemed like everything was ending.

**

So let's get back to work. Because what we need to talk about next are the lies your heart tells you when it's broken. And these are important to understand—to recognize—especially when you're sitting there sifting through so many things that are already hard enough to understand.

In the last chapter, we talked about how *quiet times* can cause your fears and insecurities to bubble up, even when you have done your best to stay busy. And at this point, I'll bet weekends are making you panic a little, aren't they? During the week, it's easy to distract yourself—but when Friday looms, and the rest of the world is getting *super* excited to settle in for two whole days of no plans—you're absolutely *dreading it.* You probably come home at the end of a long day after keeping it all together. After keeping your mind focused. And when you walk into your place, the silence is deafening. Or the toothbrushes are everywhere. Or—any other of the multitude of things you've started to feel when the silence surrounds you like that. And what you're starting to realize, too, is that *empty* and *emptiness* are two completely different beasts.

When it ended, you knew there would be holes. So—that meant there were *empty* spaces in your life that you *knew* you had to work on filling. But as you navigate this process, love, you'll find that emptiness is what comes next. And in some extra cruel twist of irony—emptiness actually *fills* empty spaces. And they get even *heavier.*

That's not part of high school science, though. At least not yet.

I hope I can find some humor to keep you laughing in this chapter. But I suspect that this one is just going to have to be me and you chatting this out. Trying to figure out what to do about this new space. Because I know what your heart is doing now. And that's what we need to talk about. It is starting to make up stories to tell you, isn't it, because it doesn't have the information it wants—it needs? And so I'll bet that it's working overtime, *filling in* those empty spaces with the kind of words that have the potential to crumble every foundation you will ever try to build anything on from here.

Since you know *exactly* what I'm talking about, I'm just going to come right out and say it.

You think *this* relationship determines your entire worth to every future one.

For some reason, you've gotten it in your head that because *this* one didn't work out—none of them will. Maybe you're—unlovable. Or damaged. Or have absolutely no idea *how* to do—this. This relationship thing. This love thing. This—*everything*. Or maybe, in that really scary part of yourself you refuse to talk about out loud—your greatest fear is that you'll be alone for your whole life. And maybe that's the way things should be— because it would be easier. Right?

So let's just address that whole thought process right now.

No. This is *so* totally not the plan for you. Or your life. Or your heart. This is not the end, this is not the beginning of the end—this is *just* the middle. The part where things *are* confusing because you're living a story that hasn't completely been told yet. I want you to know that none of those things—*none*—of those things you are telling yourself right now are true. You are not a bad person. You are not destined to be alone. You are not bad at relationships. You are not looking for something that is impossible to find. Your standards are not too high. You are not unlovable. You are not unworthy. Or unfixable. Or broken. Or any of those other lies that are bouncing around in your head and heart right now. You know what you *are*, though? I mean, really? You are human. Real. Imperfect. Learning. Trying. Growing. And what you had—was a bad experience. I need you to understand the difference. You met the wrong person for you. Right now.

And that is all.

So many of us go into relationships *knowing* we are two very different people. But—when we emerge from them—especially following an exceptionally bad experience—we somehow start blaming ourselves for everything that happened. Even though the rational part of us knows that there *are so many* collective pieces that have to fit for the "me and you" to become a healthy "us." And that's why we date. So we can learn about *who we are* in relationships—and who other people are *with us*—and whether those two things actually work when we glue them together.

I'm going to let you in on another little secret. There are quite possibly *hundreds,* or perhaps *thousands,* of people you could fall in love with. Hundreds of people you could have *chemistry* with. Hundreds of people who share similar values with you. Hundreds of people who have *all the things* you're looking for on your big laundry list for love. And whether you believe in that *one perfect person for everyone* theory or not—I think all of that still remains true. It's just that, from all those hundreds of possible matches, we add one powerful little nuance. *Our one* becomes the person who *fits into* our life in the right way at *the right time.* In a way we can't measure. And then, that person *grows with us* so they keep fitting. Does that make sense? And so that's what you need to find, love. You need to find someone who has *all those things you want* but is also standing in the same place as you.

And wants to be. And is ready.

And is willing not to *make it work*—but, quite to the contrary—*willing to work for it.*

**

One of the things your brain is going to do is ask you over and over *whether this is the right thing*. Regardless of how it all ended, or how much *say* we had in what happened, it's what our brains fixate on. If *we* were the one who ended it all, we'll wonder whether we made the right choice. Whether we should have given them more of a chance. More time. If *they* were the one who ended it, we'll second-guess whether they are waiting for us to call and make it right. Whether they meant what they said. Whether they were just going through a hard time in their lives. Whether they were pushing us away because they were scared of love.

Your brain is going to tell you a lot of things. Unfortunately, most of them won't be true. And the reason for that is because of how your brain works—what it's *designed* to do. At the core, your brain is *absolutely obsessed* with problem solving. But—all it has to work with, ever, is information it processes about what *is happening* or information it stores about what *has happened*. And since what is happening around you is often rarely enough for it to make decisions from, it draws most significantly from experience. Think of it like—a bunch of filing cabinets that have a bunch of drawers with a bunch of folders in them. And those filing cabinets and folders and drawers are filled with things *you* have put there. People. Experiences. Pain. Lessons. Goals. Timelines. Quite literally *every single thing* your eyes and ears and hands have had to work with. And learn from. And, of course, the longer you've *spent* with the things filling those drawers, the more space they take up within them. The more space they take up, generally—the more experience you have and therefore, the better you are at dealing with something.

When your brain is trying to understand something, it starts first with trying to look through all that *stuff* it's collected to see if it has anything it can work with. To help you navigate. And in situations that are *hard* to understand, or in situations we have little *experience* with—it works in overdrive—trying to formulate new connections from old data. To tell *you* a story about what happened but—that didn't happen. If that makes sense. For an image, think of a little madman pulling papers out of filing cabinets all over the place and urgently asking *does this fit? Does this go together? Could this have been the reason?*

And that is why, one of the best things you can do right now is just accept the following three things:

There was not *one* reason.

You will not *completely* understand (at least right now).

And you will learn from this, but you need to *give it time.*

I think what you need to do to help your brain and the little madman manning the filing cabinets is *create some new folders* for it to work with. And the only way you can do that is by writing all of this out. No, I really mean that. Write it out where your eyes can see it. Where you can read it out loud and your ears can hear it. And by doing that, you can *feed your brain* with new data about an old situation.

Let me be clearer.

It was never about
being *willing* to **make it work.**
It was about being willing to *work for* it.

Make sure you understand the difference.

I want you to make two lists for me. Completely stream of consciousness. And over the course of the next three or four weeks, I want you to add to both of these lists constantly. And I also want you to promise me that you won't show what you write down to anyone else. At least for right now. And that's important—because I want you to write these lists without trying to *say* things in a certain way or worrying about *how* you're saying them or *obsessing* about whether someone will judge you for how it looks. That's not what you need. And this is only about you and the truth you're sifting through right now. You ready? Two lists, here goes:

The things that didn't work. I mean it. Write them down. *Every. Single. Thing. You. Can. Think. Of.* I don't care what the reason was, or how petty it may seem, or how much it could make you *feel* high maintenance or *mean* or whatever other labels you're trying to put on yourself right now. That doesn't matter. This is about honesty. And you. And how you feel. So, get to it—write it down—*every single thing* you didn't like. That worried you. That seemed like a red flag or made your stomach flip or that you couldn't get used to. Things they said. Things they did. Things they didn't do. All of it. Write it in as much or as little detail as you want.

But write it down.

Why? Because when you need reminding that things were broken, this list is going to help you remember. And after the active hurt ends, it has another purpose, too. When you look back, what you'll find is that *these things* on *this list* will form a foundation you will use to navigate future relationships. Trust me. You'll use these things to steer. Some of them will be big things—things you will never let yourself deal with again. Others may become little trigger points that are common in many people—things you're going to have to work through with the people you love down the road. But overall, this list is what you *need most* right now. To remind you, *honestly*, that the relationship was not perfect. That *no* relationship is perfect. And since it's over, at least for now, *that* is what will carry you.

And, next, I want you to make list two.

The things that *did* work. This may seem a little strange. Hard, even. I mean—to be reflecting on what *did* work when you're trying to make sense of a breakup seems a little *insane*. Counterproductive, even. I know. But I swear this helps. While the first list will help you actively, right now, every single time you miss them—this list is more of a "down the road" benefit. The trouble is, to actually *help* you down the road, you have to write it *now*. Consider this almost like a letter to your future self.

As you write this one, it will seem like the things you're writing are starting to pull you back. Toward the person you're missing. But in a few months, what you'll find is that this list helps you in a way you'd never expected. Because what happens is *all those things* you wrote down that you *thought* were totally unique to your person—actually *weren't*. At least, not in most cases. It's just that—you put them on this list at the time because you *prioritized them* higher with this person. Which makes sense. Because relationships are a high-priority thing in our lives. But if we're honest with ourselves, which is the objective of this—*most* of what we love about people are things we *already* want to surround ourselves with. And so that probably means those qualities you wrote down are important to you in other facets of your life. From other people in your life. Do you have those qualities in your friends? Your family? I'll bet you do. And trust me—you will find them in other people you'll love down the road, too. Because those things are actually a part of who *you* are.

Does that make sense?

So build these two lists. Even though it hurts. Because I promise you, this little activity *will* teach you a lot about who *you* are. Even if it has to start by focusing on *them.*

**

I was listening to an Andy Stanley podcast today that was talking about commitment. Now, I think most of us would generally agree that commitment is a good thing, right? Well—I guess it depends on how we apply it. Like most things. But the point of Andy's argument was that when we *commit* to something we aren't *capable* of, we become unhappy.

Think about that.

When we commit to something we aren't capable of, we become unhappy.

And the reason we're unhappy, is because commitment doesn't actually *do* anything to solve problems, does it? I mean—are we any more successful at delivering a huge presentation at work or school because we're *committed* to it? Are we any more successful in the *gym* because we're *committed* to it? No—in both cases—we're not. Commitment is just a big bucket word that describes a whole bunch of other really important things. In the case of work or school, commitment really means time. Energy. Research. Reading. Writing. Patience. Growth. And *whatever else* it takes to deliver what you need to deliver. In the case of fitness? It means time and energy and choices—having to choose and prioritize what we want to accomplish over other things *we have to do.* Which means, giving up one thing to get something else.

To boil it down even further—commitment just gets us in the door. To the starting line. And it is a *great* word. And if you were *committed* to making it work, then good for you. But, you know what's better than commitment? What commitment *grows into* when it's reciprocated from both sides of a healthy relationship. *That's* when commitment changes its name and we call it more *useful* things. Like honesty. Trust. Loyalty. Communication. Kindness. Patience. Humor. Intimacy. Validation. Growth. Compassion. Acceptance. Forgiveness. *Love.*

You get me? You can't just be *committed* to having a successful relationship. And you certainly can't be the *only one* doing the committing. And that is why, to put it simply, a whole bunch of people that you will love in this life will not be right for you.

But—you *did* love them, right? And they were different—*it* was different, right? And they made you feel something. Something you had never felt before in a way you'd never felt it. And I—I can't *possibly* understand what you had. Yes, I know. I hear those words every single day from you on Instagram. And maybe you're right. So I'm not going to pretend to know the specific details of your situation. Of your life. But I *do* understand life and how it works. A lot. And that is why what you really need to do, instead of wanting to continue a love story that *at least* has that comma—if not an outright period—is start to think a little more about you. About what *you* need. About how you *have got* to find a way to understand a truth right now that is harder than even understanding the kaleidoscope of ways we learn to love each other. Harder than letting go. Harder than figuring out what happened. And why. Because this lesson is about understanding. And trusting. And making sense of all those feelings you're feeling right now that you call fear. Or sadness. Or disappointment. Or trust. Or heartache.

So here goes.

You will *never meet the right people at the wrong time.* Let me say that a different way—the way Heidi Priebe wrote it in her book *This Is Me Letting You Go*—"The people we meet at the wrong time are actually just the wrong people."

Let that sink in.

This world tells us that time—timing—is just a contributing factor. But the way I see it, timing tops the list of fundamental things that *need* to be present for a relationship to work. It's up there with all the other big things that we use to decide whether someone is right for us. And I don't believe that the right person—*the one*—will ever find us at the wrong time.

That doesn't even make sense to me.

If you and that other person would have worked—you would have worked. And what an ending teaches us, is that whether it's a forever *thing* or a just right now *thing*—*things* just weren't right. At least for now. Call it geography. Or availability. Or call it growth or healing they were working through. Or you were. But whatever you call it, just know that sometimes two wonderful people meet that are not right for each other. And are not destined to be together. And maybe the reason is just as simple as *when* they stumbled into each other's lives.

And I know that just plain old stinks—but maybe it's not as wrong as you think. Maybe—all these people we can't *quite* make sense of are put in our paths because they need to teach us something about who *we* are. Or what *we* want. Maybe they are what life uses to steer us toward some things and away from others. So maybe part of what you need to learn about all this is that *not everyone* has the potential to be a forever. And the truth is, if you're lucky—only a few of the hundreds or thousands of people you meet along the way are *ever* going to get close to holding that title. And so that means that the rest of the people you meet—they are destined to be your lessons.

And when you start doubting, I want you to remember the most important truth there is. The "right" people you meet at the wrong time are in fact, *just the wrong people*.

And it's always been *just* that simple.

**

**You
know what's
better than commitment?**
What commitment *grows into*
when it's reciprocated:
Communication.
Compassion.
Forgiveness.
Acceptance.
Validation.
Kindness.
Intimacy.
Honesty.
Patience.
Loyalty.
Growth.
Humor.
Trust.
Real.
Joy.
l

o

v

e.

10. "But Everybody Else Has *It* Already."

The pressure of time.

O riginally, I was going to write about time in the *Lies Your Heart Tells You* chapter. But as I started thinking about how I wanted to talk with you about it—I decided quickly that it deserved its own chapter. And it did because, honestly, I don't want this topic to blend in with all the other things we're talking about.

I want it to stand out.

And I want it to stand out as something *fundamental*. Something *life-changing*. Something *you* need to be more than—just aware of—but rather, *own* during this whole process.

So here goes.

I'm going to start with a number of lies you're telling yourself about time. And let's just get them all out of the way right now. You are not too young to find love—just like you are not too old to find love. You haven't run *out* of time. You have not *missed* your chance. Everybody else *does not* have it. You are not the *only one* that doesn't have someone. You are not too old to have a family. Or get married. Or buy a house. Or get divorced. Or start over. Or learn something new about yourself and what you want.

You still with me? Or are you a little stuck on *one* thing I wrote up there? One thing that you're already picking holes in—trying to document how *scientifically* or *mathematically* I am wrong? But—I *am* too old for a family. I *am* too young to find love. I *am* too old to start over. Everybody *does* have it around me.

No, love. No.

We all think that time is what we're racing. We all think we're wasting time when we aren't moving forward—when we aren't *making progress* in our love stories. Progress meaning—we meet someone. We fall madly in love. We take some fabulous trips. We get engaged. We get married. We have the house and the kids and the—*guys*. Seriously. *How* many love stories actually go like that? Especially these days? Not many I know of.

Now, if you're one of those people that followed the more traditional path, then I honestly want to say—good for you. Seriously. But—I have so many friends that have done life out of the order that the world tells us is the right way. And it's worked out beautifully for them. And maybe— maybe that is how life is going to work for you, too. But you can't see it yet because you're still so focused on the plan *you had*. When maybe, *the* plan is actually much bigger than *your* plan.

Anyway, I'm not going to go into details about what's right for you. What you should believe. What you should do. Because we all have our own set of rules that steer us. Whether you call that religion or character or upbringing—that's your call on how you do it. What I want to talk about is the pressure you put on yourself along the way. Because I'll bet one of the *first things* you do when you're standing alone again, after a relationship ends, is think you're behind.

Right?

You think—I have to start over again. It's going to take time to get to know someone. Time to trust someone. Time to build a foundation. Time to fall in love. Time to—figure out if that person *is* my one. And then, of course, if they *aren't*, you know you'll find yourself exactly where you are now, just—a little further down the road. A little more tired. A little less trusting. With a little more time that has passed. And a few more pieces of a heart that started out a lot more whole.

But I think Teddy Roosevelt said it best. *Comparison is the thief of joy.*

When you compare what you have, or where you are, to what other people have, or where they are—you are *almost always* going to come up short. Not because you actually are—but because, especially during the times of our lives we *don't* have what we want—our brains like to tell us that everyone else does. And so we look for what we *want* to see. And we see it. I *know* it's human to compare. I also know that simply telling you that *comparison* is hurting you (like, really hurting you)—*probably* won't be enough to change whether you do it. And how often you do it. But I'm still going to try. So stick with me, ok?

Someone once told me that when you are alone, it looks like everyone has someone. When you're struggling to make the rent, it looks like everyone else is buying a house. When you're getting a divorce, it looks like everyone else is getting engaged. When you're getting rejection letters from the schools or jobs of your dreams, it *looks* like everyone else is getting raises and promotions and scholarships. And, yes, when you're wanting to start a family—everyone else is already making the big fancy public announcement.

But it's *not* that everyone has what we don't.

What happens when we compare is that we *create* the reality in other people that we want to see in ourselves. Does that make sense? You see happiness and an engagement ring—but you don't know *a thing* about whether that ring stands for happy and healthy and whole. You see someone getting a big promotion at work—but you don't see *how much* that same someone struggles with how little time they have to spend with their family. You see someone having a child. But you *don't* see how many years they had to struggle to hold that child in their arms.

It's perspective. Viewpoint. When you want something and can't have it—or, *don't* have it—your longing for it makes *seeing* it in others a negative experience. And that hurts you. Holds you back. Brings you down. Makes you feel insecure and insignificant *and behind.* And that's the part we need to get past. *So* you're still swiping on dating apps. *So* you're still dating. *So* you haven't met the one. *So* you have to start over. *So* you haven't had a baby. *And?*

I don't mean that to sound harsh. I know it's hard to want something and not have it. But—I *really* want you to remember that there are *a lot* of ways this life makes things happen for us that we could never have imagined when we planned what we want. It's creative. And it weaves our experiences and strengths and weaknesses and wants and needs and desires into a perfect kaleidoscope of meaning. And while *time* is certainly at the center of getting what we want—time doesn't mean *your timeline*. Time means *timing*. The *right* timing. Ok?

And speaking of time, one more thing. This life does not have timelines for you. *You* have timelines for you. And I guarantee if you go back and figure out when and where those timelines were set—chances are, it *wasn't* actually you that set them. It was the world. It was your parents. It was your friends. It was where you thought you needed to be by now based on where you saw everyone else. I mean—is it possible that you have measured your whole life with *someone else's* measuring stick? And is that really what you want—what was right for someone else when *they* chose it? Ok. So maybe it *was you* that decided by twenty-eight you wanted to be married, and at thirty-five you still haven't gotten close. Maybe *it was you* that had dreams to be the young parent—to have your two and a half kids by thirty-two. Maybe it *was you* that decided you were going to be married for a lifetime. That you'd defy the odds. That you were different. That *they* were different.

Look, I hate to break this to you, but there's something else I need you to understand. Andy Stanley also coined this little nugget. *You* are different. But your *situation* is not. Trust me. We're all out there struggling to be who we thought we were going to be. And that is why, when things like this happen, we *have* to take the time to reflect on how that adjusts our plan. Because when things *change, things* change. Does that make sense? If you're following a path and *everything* on that path is telling you it is not your path, *you have to get off that path*. If you keep picking the same kind of person because they are your *type* and your *type* hasn't worked for you yet—then *you need a new type*. And if you keep making the same mistakes over and over and over—then you need to stop and reflect. On who you are. On what you're doing. On *why*.

And then—yes—you *have* to adjust.

No one is going to do this for you. No, really—they aren't.

You have to adjust your life and your direction and your choices. *You* have to work on your perspective and your viewpoint and your attitude. And while you're doing all that, you have to give yourself permission to *change* who you thought you were and what you *thought* you wanted. Because I'm just going to say it—maybe your road looks nothing like the road you're on and had always thought you wanted. Maybe your road is transforming. Into the one you *never* knew you *always* wanted. And needed. And isn't that so much better?

**

I don't want you to spend your whole life rushing to chase after people who are running from you. I don't want you to keep struggling to keep up with the pace your friends are setting in the races they are running in their own lives. *That is how you get tired*, love. And when you get tired, you don't live your best life. You aren't happy. You aren't patient. You don't bring the right *self* into the space you occupy. You don't have the joy and energy to invest in what you want. What you need. *So—don't.* Don't get caught up running after (or running from) all those things the world tells you that you should be running after. Or from. This is not you against everyone else. It never has been. And it is not you *against* time, either.

You have to
adjust your life
and your direction
and your choices.

You have to work
on your perspective
and your viewpoint
and your attitude.

And *you* have to
give yourself
permission
to change
who you
thought
you were
and what
you *thought*
you really wanted.

This is (and has always been) a journey *you* are taking *for* you.

There are big questions to answer in this life. You know that. But I feel like this chapter would be incomplete without addressing perhaps one of the biggest. And I think it fits somewhat neatly within this chapter on time—simply because these two things are often in direct contradiction with each other. And most of us don't even realize it.

We think time is ticking by and for some reason we can't explain, the universe just isn't sending us the love story we are looking so long and hard for. We love. And lose. And love. And lose. And all the while, keep searching this world over for someone who just *knows* how to love us. And maybe that's the problem. Right there. The belief that this person just magically exists somewhere in the universe—and it is our job to find them. But I think that's just plain old wrong. I don't think the right person is hiding from us. I think—most of us don't *see* them because *we* don't even know where to look. And the reason for that is simple.

We don't know what we are actually looking for.

At the heart of every good love story are two people who know the answer to the one most important love question there is:

Do you know how you need to be loved?

That's it. That's the one that changes the course of your whole life. And every single person that you'll ever love within it. Regardless of where you are on your journey, you *need* to answer that question for yourself. I mean it. Maybe start by making a list. Just start randomly jotting down anything that comes to you. *How* do you want to be loved? What does it look like? What does it sound like? What would someone do—or say—to be a good partner for you? And, just as importantly, what kinds of things would they *not do? Not* say?

Look—you *better start figuring out* the answer to those questions. And soon. Because if you don't know what you're *really* looking for in someone else, then tell me, love—how on earth are you ever going to know when you find them? And so that's what I mean when I say maybe time isn't the real problem here. Maybe the real problem is we've all spent far too long searching for someone else—when we actually had no idea who we were, either.

So I'll just leave you with this. And take it for what you will.

The love you need is a language that only you speak and *you have got to know how to translate that for the people who want to love you.* It's not their job to just know. It's your job—to *say it out loud.* Love is not about finding someone who knows how to love you perfectly. Love is about finding someone who *cares enough* to *want* to know how to love you perfectly.

Make sure you get that right, ok?

**

So here's the lesson. At least for this chapter. Time—is complicated. It can be on your side or against you. It can make you feel like you are always rushing to keep up, or it can slow to make you think absolutely nothing is moving forward at all. It can hurt you and heal you—make you remember, and forget. But mostly? Mostly—time humbles you. It humbles you in a way you will never expect and won't think you need and will never see coming. It gives you these incredible chances to love someone—but the opportunity to know how to *heal* from loving someone, too. You'll get to be the one with the crazy beautiful love story sometimes—and others, time will fade you into the blur of everybody else. Of waiting. Of comparing. Of learning.

If you
don't know what
you are really looking for in someone else—
then *how* are you ever going to know
when you actually find it?

Take it all.

Take the good and the bad and the beautiful and every single thing in-between. Because with it, time teaches *you to see.* What matters and what doesn't. When an end is a beginning. And when an end is truly an end. And trust me when I say—you're going to get a bit of it all. You're going to feel like you've got it all handled and you're completely lost. You'll feel like you have it all figured out and like you have absolutely no idea what you're doing. You're going to change your heart and your eyes and your mind and your type and your footsteps. You're going to fit in and stand out, be loved and broken. And I can't promise you how much of it all you're going to get, but I can promise you one thing.

You are not going to *not* have something because you don't have it by now. Time will teach you that. But until it does, do your best to remember this: the people who are meant to *grow* with you will *go* with you.

So learn to trust the no as much as you do the yes.

**

The people **who are meant** to grow with you—
will *go* with you.

11. "Bodies, Faces, and Shopping Sprees."

How loss changes you, and why you change because of it.

'm sitting here, at a coffee shop, listening to music. I'm at one of my favorite writing places—parked at one of the tables outside with my laptop. It's late summer, and the air has a slight breeze. Usually I don't write to music—but today, I needed some inspiration to kick off this chapter. Eric Church never disappoints. *Record Year* is on in my headphones.

One of the things I absolutely love about music is the way life changes how it sounds. You can hear a song when you're in one place in your life and it won't mean a *thing* to you. But, if that same song floats into your headphones or speakers during other times—it completely transforms into *your* song. The one where the whole universe is *quite literally* speaking to you through someone else's voice.

You've felt that, right? I know you have.

Sometimes it's as simple as the chills you get on the back of your neck. Others, it's that *stop you in your tracks* feeling when you're listening alone in the car. But that's what I love—how music can teach us a million different things about ourselves depending on *when* we hear it.

Now, maybe you aren't a country fan, but either way—Eric's song ended up becoming the impetus for this entire chapter. I know. Crazy. But his words about the end of a love story—and how we keep score—are speaking to me.

When a relationship ends, we are each forced into a highly personal, highly *critical* assessment of *who* we are and *what* we're not. We've already talked about that—how blame carries us during these vulnerable times. But, in this particular place of questions and chaos and hurt and healing—that same "blame" can actually end up pushing you toward something *really* good. If you learn to use it wisely. And what I want to talk about in this chapter is just that. Change.

How loss changes *you*. And why *you* change because of it.

And before we get started, I just want you to know that how you *do* this, love, will determine *a very large part* of how you carry what happened to you. After this.

So here's how it works.

**

The first thing we do is crash into the *change everything* phase. We do it somewhat like a, excuse my cliché, but—bull in a china shop. What I mean is, we don't put a lot of thought into what we do. Into the choices we're making. And why. It's an equation of—we're hurting. We don't want to hurt. We want the hurt to stop. We think we might know a way to make it stop. So we try that thing. It works for a while. The hurt comes back. And then we try something else.

The first phase is a bit of a spiral. Chaotic, even.

In this place, we look for the quick fixes—the things we know full well aren't going to heal us, but we still want them anyway. For distraction. Avoidance. To boost our self-confidence. To make sure if we run into our *person* on the street they know *exactly* what they're missing. Right? (You *totally* do that. Don't even try to deny it.)

Anyway, most of us tend to start with the things we didn't—or couldn't— do when we were in the relationship. And one of the quickest ways to accomplish that is, yes, you guessed it. *Spending money.* Maybe it's something as simple as a new outfit—or, maybe it's a new car. Maybe you redecorate your bedroom. Or your whole house. Maybe you change your style completely. Or—maybe you pack up and move yourself somewhere completely new. Or change your job. Or buy a plane ticket to one of your bucket-list places with absolutely no other plan.

Am I close?

Side note—I know some of you are going to read this little description of phase one and buying things and say *I didn't do that. That wasn't me.* Maybe you'll even think buying things or spending money is too materialistic and definitely not a healthy part of healing. And—you'd be right. Buying things and spending money has nothing to do with being healthy—and I'm not saying it's the roadmap to get *you* through this.

What I am saying is—if you're doing it, it's ok for now. Give yourself a pass. Healing doesn't begin in the place we actually start to feel better—healing begins in the place we *figure out* that we've been doing something wrong. And realizing *that* is what gets us to the actual starting line.

So the trouble with this first *change everything* phase, love, is while it's super distracting (in a great way) for a short period of time, it doesn't *really* last. Well, actually, it outright *doesn't* last. And because it doesn't, most of us transition quickly to the second phase. The one where we have an urgent desire to more permanently change *everything* about, well, yes—our bodies. Because, as we are deciding through this process, our bodies *must* be the only currency we have to offer in love. And that goes for both the relationship we've lost, as well as any that are coming in the future. Right?

Wrong. But, we'll get to that in a minute.

In this second phase, we focus a little more on lasting results. We're generally done with the quick fixes, and know—in some *starting to be rational* part of us—that we *do* need to grow from this. So that's when we join the gym. Or sign up for super endurance races. Or, maybe, get plastic surgery. Or lose weight. Or grow out our hair. Or cut our hair. Or start saving money. Or—a million other things.

The trouble with *this phase,* quite similar actually, to the first, is the way we end up thinking about it. We somehow convince ourselves that *once we have that, we'll feel this.* Meaning—we think we can *quite literally* transform our bodies and lives, and our hearts and minds will just naturally follow. We think that once we have the surgery done or the marathon accomplished or the weight lost—that things are going to be different. That *we* are going to be different.

But that's not exactly what happens, is it?

What happens when we accomplish all those things outwardly is—we accomplish all those things outwardly. And sure, maybe our bodies look different. Maybe we're happier with ourselves. Maybe people give us more attention. But—as we all eventually find out, the mind and heart bouncing around inside that shiny new body with the new clothes or house or geography or job— *they* are still very much the same.

And *they* still have the same old worries, don't they? The same old insecurities? The same trigger points and behaviors and scars and baggage? You know what I mean, love. *They* still look in the mirror with you and tuck you into bed at night telling you the same old stories. The ones the rest of the world will never hear. And you will never tell them.

And that's phase three.

The place where we realize (and then figure out how to admit to ourselves) that *because* we've spent so much time working on *just* what the world gets to see—we've missed out on the opportunity to *really* heal that part of us that the world doesn't. And so *this* is the place where we finally decide that all the things we can buy and do to our bodies and lives to make people *see* us differently don't really mean a thing if we don't learn to see ourselves differently. And that—*that*—is where real growth happens. From that place. Where we start to reflect. Ask for help. Get a counselor. Meditate. Open up. Heck—write a whole darn book. And *that* is what I want us to work on in this chapter. Phase three.

Oh, and one other thing? Because I'm not you and I don't know your situation—I'm going to tell you right now that I do not have the answer for how *you* need to learn these things. But I do have some of the things you are probably going to end up learning.

And that's a start, I think. Knowing where you're going—that's a start.

**

After this, you will know more about the way people work. Right now, you're still using labels for all those things that happened to you. It's raw. I get it. So you're still calling it heartbreak. Betrayal. Differences you couldn't accept. Lies. Endings. Anger. Hurt. Trust. Or—maybe just *plain old compli-cated.* But whatever the case, and whatever you're calling it—because you're still so early in your healing, you're going to believe that what I meant by that line is—*people are bad.* And they can't be trusted. And love ends. And people cheat. And you're going to be alone. And you deserved this. And—

. . . that is *not* what I mean.

What I mean is, after this, you will understand the *different* ways people work. And I mean this more than the cliché little bumper-sticker version of it—but *people aren't perfect.* And we are *all* different and *all* the same. In a really good way. We all bring different experiences and backgrounds and hurt and lessons and hang-ups and desires. But then, we all say things we don't mean and mean things we don't say and think we're ready for things we're not and that we're not ready for things we are. We slip up and pretend and tell little white lies. We want to get better and be better but aren't quite sure how to do it. We all paint on our best self to catch someone and then show them our real self once we've caught them. We're all works in progress. Trying to do the best we can with the best we've got. And *that* is what I mean. You will understand more about *the people* part of people. And how, at the core, they just *are* who they are. And that's just the way it is.

Healing
does not
begin in
the place
we start
to feel better—
healing
begins in
the place
where we
figure out
**what we've
been doing wrong.**

Which brings me to the next thing.

Even if you trust *them* less, you trust yourself more. I know. You don't believe me on this one. But *this* is so simple it's not actually going to take much to explain it to you.

After this, you're going to know what your intuition sounds like. What it *feels* like when your gut is talking to you—when your *instincts* are trying to tell you something. Good or bad. And, because you'll know what those things look and sound and feel like—you're going to *start* being better at *owning* how you really feel. You *won't* ignore your feelings. You won't let *other people* ignore your feelings. And you most definitely will not let other people *tell you* how you should feel. You just wake up one day and you're done with that whole game. Your feelings are how you feel. Period. Whether they are justified. Or make sense. Whether they are "right" or "wrong."

You. *Own.* Them.

So—when you feel something, you actually start to take the time to think about why you're feeling that way. No more downplaying or ignoring or saying *it's ok* when it is *not* ok.

And *that* goes hand in hand with finding the right people. And the next lesson.

You realize you can't change people—and actually, you don't want to. We *all* start out wanting to change people. We don't *ever* admit that, but we do. We think—this person has *just* about all the things we want—but not quite. And we can *work* on those.

Guys—people may change. They *may* even change for you. But trust me when I say that change will never happen because *you* ask them for it. Or give them ultimatums. Or try to make someone understand how much what they do or don't do *affects* you. Or your kids. Or your life. Change happens when *the person that needs to change* decides that they *want to.* The end.

You understand that, right?

Well, you will. I promise. And once you do, the great irony is that in real-izing you can't change others, it actually starts to change you. In a truly beautiful way. Because *that* is the point you start to *really* evaluate the relationships—and the kind of relationships—that you let into your life. And just the same as you no longer want a partner that's a project—who you have to *make* fit—you also start to see that beautiful other side you never even realized existed. That it's *about them,* too. And even more than just your part, you start to *really want* to give other people the opportu-nity to find the people that fit *their* lives, too. Even if it's not you.

And I guess that's where it starts hurting a little less when things end. I don't mean it to sound so simple—because it's definitely *not* simple until you actually get there. But once you're there, this one just makes everything so much clearer. So much easier. Because, truthfully, things will either work. Or they won't. And time will take care of that. Now, just to be clear—I'm definitely not saying that relationships don't take effort. Give and take. Compromise. Patience. Growth. And a whole bunch of other words in that same category. Because they do. A lot of it. What I'm saying is, *wanting to work on things* is different than wanting to *change someone.* In one case, you're doing it together. In the other? You're wanting to shout at a kite and expect it to fly higher. Does that make sense?

You'll get here. You will get to the place where you *just* start living your life and enjoying the process. And that means you accept things for what they are. And especially, for what they're not. You will get to the place where you just hope that the example you set *for other people* will be enough for them to change the parts of themselves they *need* to. Or want to. And when they *don't* change and it *does* negatively affect your life—you start to have that clarity you need to make the critical choices. You stop waiting. And you choose—willingly—what is (or is not) right for you. Based entirely upon what you *know* to be true. And *not* what you hope will one day be true *if* someone changes.

Let me put that another way. What I mean is—you learn to base *your decisions* on *your truth.*

And not someone else's *maybes.*

**

I remember one of my friends telling me, in the midst of my post-breakup hurt (Remember Chicago airport guy?) that I had the *power* to control how *I* felt about things. In concept, that made perfect sense to me. In practice, it made absolutely none. She had explained that while yes—things happen *to* us; we each have the power to decide what those things *mean* to us when they happen. I remember *hearing* what she had said—and just being happy she had obviously figured out some grand secret of the universe. One that, clearly, I had not.

We typically look at emotions as something reactive. Meaning, we experience something in our lives and we respond *to* it. I always used to think it was about controlling the experience—and *that* is where the peace came from. In the predicting. The preparing. The somehow getting good enough at life that we're able to see things coming in advance or navigate them better *while* they are happening. And sure, maybe in some cases that actually does help. But I think what she meant, and what I've now found to be true, is that it's never actually been about the *experience*. It's about how *we* choose to see that experience. Like she said.

Bad things happen. Unexpected things happen. Things you are not prepared for and don't want and would never choose for yourself happen. But that's life. And like many wise people have said—*life doesn't get better*. We do. And I think *that* is what she meant. Inner peace isn't about controlling what happens to you. Or who happens to you. Inner peace is about controlling what *you do* with what happens to you. It's how we choose to see it—what filing cabinet you choose to put it in. It's the *grace* you find in the moments when people aren't perfect and don't show you their best selves. It's the kindness you muster when you're a little too far behind another heart that wants you so badly to catch up. And the strength you find when you realize an end is necessary. But hard.

We don't have to be good at all this stuff. But we *do* have to figure out what works for us. And that's what I mean. Inner peace is a balance that each of us has to find for ourselves. And there are a million books and a million podcasts and a million little nuggets your friends and family are going to share with you about how *they* found their inner peace. But this is personal. And what works for someone else may have *nothing to do* with what will work for you. You're going to have to do a *lot* of exploring and experimenting to figure it all out, and that takes time. But I'll tell you—while you're experimenting with exactly how to get it all right (and keep it there)—you will learn quickly how it can go *wrong*. And you will become a master at being able to identify the things that *take* your inner peace away. And so that's where you start.

And this awareness just makes you—*more cautious*—of who you let into your circle. But—not in a lack of trust way. More like a *conscious* way. You want good energy. People who build you up. Make you laugh. Teach you something. Not—people who constantly take and never give. So through this, you'll find that when a certain kind of person or a certain type of situation starts to upset that balance—you steer clear of it. At least, when you can.

And since you understand yourself a little more now, you start to make different choices, too. You stop saying maybe when you want to say no. You stay home when you don't want to go out. You say what you think— what you mean—even if someone might not like it. You show people who you are. *Really.*

You live *your* truth.

And I'll tell you—truth is the foundation that all inner peace is built on. *That* is the secret. Which brings me to the more strategic part of controlling your inner peace.

**

Not taking everything so personally. I know. This is whopper of a topic. But I'm actually not going to spend a lot of time on it, because it all boils down to a pretty simple fact.

This is not all about you.

Remember back when we talked about the lies your heart tells you when it's broken? Well, that's part of what I mean here. But I'm going to say it again, just so it echoes. *Nothing* is *entirely* your fault. Ok? When someone can't love you, or doesn't, or won't—that is not a reflection on your ability to be loved. Or your value. Or your worth. Or whatever other currency you're trying so hard to attach to it.

People make choices every single day that are almost entirely based upon themselves. I mean it. Look it up. Statistically, psychologically, habitually—we *all* take other people's choices personally. Like it has something to do with what we do or don't bring to the table. But—I swear that is only the smallest part of it—the *majority* of people's decisions are based entirely upon them. And where they are (or aren't) in their lives.

People say things. And do things. And want things. They screw up. And act on impulses and make stupid decisions when they're tired or emotionally drained. We all do. We're not perfect. And I'm not saying that you shouldn't reflect on what you learn from the situations you go through. About the two of you and, of course, yourself.

All I'm saying is that we say *my life* a heck of a lot more than we say *our lives*.

You get it?

**

There are *so many* more things I want you to know about change and growth. Things like—you're going to understand loneliness better. But in a good way. And it's going to make sense that while being alone is hard— it's much harder to feel alone *with* someone else. I could go on and on in this chapter, but—I'm going to stop here and let you really think about what *you* need for *your* life. It's great that you want to change—it really is. But real change isn't defined by what change produces—real change is defined by what drove the desire to change in the first place. Does that make sense? Are you changing yourself *for* someone else? *Because* of someone else? To *get* something? To *have* something? To *be* something? And why do you think changing will give you what you think you don't have now? Who made you believe that? Is it true?

Anyway, maybe you don't know those answers yet. But I encourage you to explore those questions. And what you really want from this whole experience. From yourself. From this life. And as you make choices— *especially* when those choices mean changing who you are and what you want and who you're with—make sure you're choosing what is best for *your life.* For *your* happiness. Because, yes, like I said—that *is* really what matters. The *you* part.

If you're not happy, you *cannot* give your best self to anyone else. So, at the risk of sounding like an airline safety presentation—I have to say it.

Put your own oxygen mask on first.

No, really. Do it. You actually *owe* that to yourself.

**

***Real* change**
is not measured
by what it produces—
it is measured by
what drove the desire
to change things
in the first place.

12. "I Will *Never* Love Like This Again."

Yes, you will love like this again.

I didn't plan to write *this* chapter. It kind of just—happened. Today I posted a *small* excerpt from this book—the draft manuscript—on Instagram. I coupled it with this little watercolor photo I found of two people, and all it said was *You. Will. Love. Like. **This.** Again.* In the caption, like I usually do, I posted some thoughts on just that. From *this* book. And it went crazy. Comments and messages and likes. Times—*fifty thousand or so?*

Now, I typically don't use those kinds of metrics to measure the success of what I write. At least, I try not to—because that is certainly *not* how I want to measure impact. Or value. But—I definitely watch what you do with what I post to see what you resonate with. And I read all the comments. Always. And you know, most of the comments this morning, on this particular post, were you tagging your friends and telling them to "read the caption." The rest talked about how timely it was—how much you needed to hear just those words. How much—you wish you'd known that truth a little sooner.

Most were like that. But one comment stood out to me, because it did *not* say that.

This is the comment someone wrote under my post this morning about hope: *"No. I won't. I won't **ever** be able to love someone again. I don't trust in all of this anymore."*

Wow.

I thought a lot about what I wanted to say—and how I wanted to say it. Part of me even considered sending a direct message to this hurting soul rather than responding publicly. But, in the end, I decided that more than a few of you probably needed to hear this. And feel like this. I know I have. So I chose to keep my response public.

And as I typed it, I realized something about this whole healing process that maybe I had overlooked a little. I mean—we don't *only* have doubts about ourselves and the reasons the relationship we're healing from ended, do we? One of the biggest doubts that settles in *after* the active hurt has settled down is—*exactly*—what this single human from somewhere on this earth wrote on a post today about this book. Maybe one day she will know how much that single thought contributed to something that will hopefully help a lot more people.

I love how that kind of thing works.

What I ended up writing to her was this: "I understand it may feel that way. But that's just what *healing* feels like. Trust me, you *will* find someone who will make you believe again. But until that happens, just go easy on yourself, and all the things you did (and do) when love was leading you."

So, let's talk about it. That doubt. How you think—how maybe in some way *we all think*—that life doesn't know what it's doing when things like this happen. We doubt. *A lot.* That there is a purpose for loving some-one—and then losing them. For *having* to go through pain and loss. For trusting. But mostly, we doubt that *we* can ever—will ever—*want* to ever do it all over again.

And even if we did, that it would work.

But guys? Trust me when I say: you will. I will. We *all* will.

**

I *get* that one of the last things you want to believe when hard times are here is that good times are coming. Well, maybe it's not just that. Because it's not that you *don't* want to believe, is it? It's just that—gosh—it's hard. All this stuff. All these questions. All this—getting used to a new life *without* the someone you thought was going to be doing it with you.

What you're carrying right now—it's heavy. And maybe that's the thing about healing that's really hard to understand until you're already in the midst of it. When we're carrying heavy stuff, we get tired. And being tired makes us do and see things very differently than when we're healthy and happy and whole. We only have one bank of emotional energy to draw from. And when we spend *all* of that emotional energy *lugging* around heavy stuff, it takes the joy out of life for a little while. Not because *joy* isn't there, but—because we're too tired to even look for it. And so we don't. And then we don't see it. And that hurts. And frankly, being exhausted is no *fun,* is it? So, in one of the most human actions we ever take—we *gravitate* toward the people and things that make that hurt stop. That carry some of our baggage for us for a while. It's nice. It feels good. But it's just a Band-Aid, love. Temporary. And while it may work for a little while, it will *not* work forever. And that is why *you* need time to heal before you go and throw yourself into something else. Before you ask *anyone* to help you carry what is already too heavy for you.

A healthy relationship is built from *two* healthy hearts. **Two.**

Look—I know that some of you have been carrying what you've been carrying for a lot longer than you ever imagined you would. And I also know some of you are devouring this book because it all went down just a few days ago. Or weeks ago. And because it's new, you're hoping somewhere within these pages is a little roadmap to help you get through it. Well. I certainly hope that's true.

But—now is the time to talk about *one last lesson* in all of this.

And this one—forces you to look forward instead of back.

Because this is about how it will feel. One day.

When you are ready to love again.

Because you will be.

I promise.

**

I could tell you a lot of things right now, before we get into all of this. Some of them might make you feel a whole lot better. They might be things you could latch onto and roll around in your head to calm your racing thoughts. I could tell you sure, he needs time. Or she needs space to figure out what she wants. I could tell you he'll regret it. Or she'll change. Or he is making the biggest mistake of his life.

But I'm not going to. And I'll tell you why.

Because I *don't* know your situation. And I don't know *theirs*. And so anything I could say to *make you feel* better wouldn't be based on anything real. About your life. About your relationship. And that's simply not fair to you. And trust me, love, if it's not real, it is *not* going to help you right now. I do have something to tell you, though. And maybe down the road it *will* make you feel better. I mean, you can certainly latch onto it.

Whatever the reason was that things had to end, they ended.

I know. Not what you're looking for. And definitely not what you wanted to hear. But that is truly the *only* thing that matters right now. Yes, you may very well be the exception to every single rule there is. You may defy the odds. You guys may end up working things out and be together in the end with a great story to tell. There are a lot of ways this can go. But I don't know that story right now. And neither do you. And *that* is a story only time can write.

Everyone who crosses our paths ends up teaching us something. And you know, it's not always the ones that are with us the longest that teach us the most. Sometimes the most powerful lessons are also the ones we get the shortest time to experience. Look—if you're lucky, you're going to be on this planet for a long time. You're probably going to meet a ton of people. A handful that you're going to love in some way. And maybe—a few more than you'll *fall* in love with. So no matter *how* what you're going through ends up working out, I need you to realize something. While everyone teaches us—temporary people sometimes teach us the most permanent lessons.

So just for the sake of what I am trying to explain to you, I'm going to say that the person you're healing from was a *temporary* part of your life. Yes, I realize you may have been married. I realize you may have grown up together. I realize you may have kids or have *really thought they would be there through it all*. But here's the hard truth. They aren't here right now, are they? At least not in the way you thought they'd be. Or wanted them to be. So—they are teaching you a permanent lesson. And it's time you realize what that was:

What you deserve most is what you don't have right now.

I'm going to let that one sink in. I'm going to let you start to think of all the rebuttals. The things I don't understand about your situation. You. Them.

Got your list?

Ok, now let me explain. What you deserve *most* is not this feeling. Not this confusion. Not this sadness. This hurt. I mean, all love stories are a little complicated, sure—but not like this. You deserve someone who knows what they've got when they've got it. You deserve someone who isn't quoting "it's a bad time" or "I need to find myself." You deserve a partner. Someone who works *with* you to get what you both want. You deserve someone who will *grow* with you. Who doesn't let you walk away. Who fights for you. Who wants the same things you do. Who trusts you. Who isn't worried about geography or you affecting their ten-year plan. You deserve someone who thinks you *are* their ten-year plan. You deserve someone who supports what you love, even if they don't really get it. Who gives you room to grow. To change your mind. To adjust your schedule. To makes mistakes. You deserve someone who stands by you, even when they fundamentally disagree with what you're saying. You deserve someone who doesn't want to change you—but somehow inspires you to be the absolute best version of yourself you could ever be.

You deserve someone who *thinks* they don't deserve you.

Do you get that?

So this is the part where I tell you to stop making excuses. Stop telling yourself you could have made it work. That they could have changed. That there *were* good times. I mean, of course there were good times. You wouldn't have been with them if they weren't a good person. If you didn't have fun. Didn't have chemistry. Didn't have—*something incredible* that you built everything else on. And that's what you need to understand. What you *deserve* most is what you don't have right now. And I'll tell you why. Because you deserve a love that doesn't have to leave you to miss you. That doesn't have to end to continue. And maybe if you started with that, you just may be that much closer to finding the love story you keep searching for.

And haven't found yet.

**

We risk a lot in the blind faith we'll get the love we search this world for. And as we bounce into all those hearts we love along the way—we learn. A lot. About what we want. Need. Can't accept. I guess it's a lot of trust mixed with some luck and opportunity. Something like—planned trial and error. If that makes any sense. But the way I figure it, there are exactly four kinds of people you'll love in this lifetime. And each and every one will teach you—some more painfully than others—but also push you closer and closer to what you're looking for.

So here they are. The magic four.

One. You'll get the people that ignite that spark within you—that make you feel like you've always dreamed of feeling. That make you feel warm and happy and *seen*. But that—when you're really honest with yourself—lack the core qualities you need in a good partner. In a lifetime kind of love. They are the ones *who hurt you.*

Two. The ones that have exactly what you *think* you're looking for—but for whatever reason, the timing is just off. You're too far ahead, or maybe they are—but you're just not standing in the same place in this life. You'll probably hold on a little too long to them, too—hoping the universe will let you catch up to each other. These are the relationships *that hurt you both.*

Three. The ones who seem to have every single thing on your list. And on paper, you should love them like you've never loved anyone before. But for some reason you just can't explain—you don't. Or can't. And they are the ones *you* hurt.

And finally, four. There's *the* one. The one who holds your hand without holding you back. The one that is ready for you—the one *you* are ready for. And *that* is the one that makes the journey through the other three worth it. And *that* is what, if you're reading this book, you still have to look forward to.

And trust me, you need them all. You really do.

So let me just tie up this chapter with a message to that sweet human that inspired it. And to you.

You. Will. Love. Like. That. Again.

At certain points in my life, that is *all* I wanted someone to tell me. Yes—you will find happiness again. Yes—you will be ok and yes things will settle down and yes they will *absolutely* make sense again.

But I want you to know something else, too.

Actually, you won't find *that* kind of love again. You will find something better. But when that time comes, I *promise* that you won't believe you have ever loved like that before. And that's the beauty of how love works. Because every single time we do it, it works *that much better*. Goes that much deeper. Lasts that much longer. So don't you dare stop loving just because you loved once. Just because this time *hurt* you. Just because you met someone who wasn't ready for you. Or wasn't your person. Or couldn't see your value for what it *is*. Or wasn't your forever.

Keep your heart open and *let love in again*. When you're ready.

Because there is always room. And there will always be someone who is worth it.

And remember, if you don't trust again—don't love again—*they* get to keep your future *and* your past. And that seems like a pretty high price to pay. Doesn't it?

**

You. **Will.** Love. Like. *That.* Again.

13. "It Ended for a Reason."

Most of the questions, some of the answers.

O k. So we're almost done here. And I think this is the real chapter you've been waiting for. The one with the answers. The *why* this had to happen. The *what could have possibly* caused this? The—do they miss me? Are they coming back? Am I going to be alone for my entire life? What's wrong with me? And the all-encompassing—*why* does this keep happening to me and *how* can I be sure next time won't be like this time?

Take a deep breath, love. And let's start with the basics.

No one person is perfect for any other one person. Can we at least agree on that? Good. Now—because we can start from that point, let's also agree that every relationship comes with work. Some are harder than others—but all of them take some shaping. Some polishing. Some— patience and time and growth—to make them work in the best way for you and that other person. And work—*work* isn't always a collective effort. It's not always a "let's work on us" effort. And this isn't a book about working on the us, anyway—it's a book about working on the you. So, I'm not going to get into how you work through something with someone else. What I want to focus on—and hope you will too—is what *you need to learn about yourself* from this experience. And trust me—it's probably not what you think. Especially right now, in the trenches of the active hurt. So let me be clear. What you should *not* take away from this ending is any of the following:

That you are hard to love. That you will be alone your whole life. That it was all your fault. That you deserved it. That people always treat you badly and it's never going to change. That you're not good enough. Pretty enough. Smart enough. Confident enough.

I mean, those are probably things you're going to tell yourself. At least a little in some part of this process—but they are *not* the real focus of healing. Those things—those things are fears. And fears are not what you need to build a foundation on in this life. Especially a foundation that someone else is going to one day want to stand on to build a love story with you.

So let's really get to the heart of the issue. You. And let's *explore who you are* in the relationships you choose to spend your life in. Because, if you're honest with yourself—and I hope you will be—*you* are the common denominator of every relationship you have ever been in. Or ever will be. Which means—to really look at how and what you might need to learn from all of this, you *have got* to explore who you are when you are with someone else. Do you know your insecurities? Do you know your vulnerabilities? Do you know the things you constantly do, over and over, that might contribute in some way to an unhealthy foundation? Do you know what things you still carry with you from the past that could *affect* someone else in the future?

You need to, love. And these are hard questions. I get it. None of us want to admit that we play any part in the downfall of anything. Especially when it's someone and something we loved. It is much easier to blame someone else than it is to admit, like we just agreed, that all relationships take work. That we *have to be* our best self to build our best us. So whether you agree that what happened could have been part your fault or not, I still want us to explore this.

So stay with me, ok?

You are the *one thing* that remains constant no matter who you're in a relationship with or what happens *in that relationship*. Now, does that mean what happened is all your fault? Absolutely not. That's not the way blame works. But—everything from what you bring to a relationship when you start out to how you navigate it in the end says a lot about who you are. And I don't think this book would be complete without a chapter on—at least—reflecting on that. The *who you are* and *what you need to learn from this* moving forward.

**

All relationships are, by their very definition—partnerships. To me, that looks a lot like a seesaw. A seesaw is never completely balanced, but instead, is shifting back and forth constantly when the person on one side kicks a little harder off the ground. It picks the other person up—until they touch down and do the same thing. Sometimes it's not a drastic difference. Remember when you were little and you used to try to perfectly balance with someone on a seesaw? You got close, but it never worked perfectly. I think relationships are like that. They are—never fifty-fifty. Never. Maybe they are eighty-twenty. Or seventy-thirty. Or sixty-forty. Or forty-nine–fifty-one. But they are *never* equal. One person is always carrying a little more than the other at any one time. And then it shifts. Rebalances. So the person carrying the heavier load doesn't get tired.

Do you get that?

So—what I need you to reflect on is what percent you were carrying. This time. Was it all of it? Or did you accidentally make them carry it all and not even realize it? Guys. This is not a perfect science. You're going to make mistakes. But what I need you to realize through this process is what your *trend* is. And what your piece *should be.* Meaning—do you always carry the majority of the load? Bend over backward to try to give the person you're with absolutely everything? And why? Do you think you *need* to do that for them to love you? Or—do you always look for someone that will—at the risk of sounding cliché again—*save* you? From your past? From yourself? Because I'll tell you, neither of those are what you build a solid foundation on.

Neither of those are a *partnership.*

So I want you to make a list. (Yes, another list.) Of the things you did to build the relationship. To nurture it. To keep it fun or interesting. I want you to think about the things you did—little and substantial—to challenge the person you were with. Because that's an essential thing. If we choose to spend our lives with someone, we need to find someone who will grow *with us* constantly. So—how did you help them grow? What did you teach them? Were you accepting when *they* wanted to grow? Especially in a situation or scenario that made little sense to you? That you didn't agree with? Didn't understand? And—how did you push them out of their current safe boundaries? What did all of that look like?

Do some thinking, love. And then some math.

What did the seesaw look like? And why?

**

Most of us get how this all works. We get that people aren't puzzle pieces and they don't just fit together when it comes to love. What happens is—we define this magical list of things that are super important to us, and we look for those things in the people we choose to spend our lives with. Since we can't manufacture the perfect match—we end up sifting through the people that cross our paths to find the "almosts." And then we spend time getting to know those people. We spend time figuring out whether they are—actually—the right matches for us. We see those big things in them—that's what attracts us initially. And what we learn— slowly—are the details. The ones that add to—or detract from—the big picture when it comes to whether they fit in our lives.

Now I think—what also happens—is this is the place we start making excuses for the people we love. Maybe it's not all entirely bad, either. Because we have to accept the flaws that come as part of just us being real. But—after we've noticed that someone has some of those critical things we want, we get attached. Those are the edge pieces of the big picture. As we learn things we don't like, we cast them aside a bit because we realize in some parts of our heads and hearts that it's easier to keep what we have than to get what we don't.

Starting over is hard.

Look, love—your job in all this was the experience. It was the loving. It was the learning how many ways that heart of yours can love someone else. The figuring out who you were—and who you were with them. And what you got to do with that. The "them" part—that was their job. Who they were with you and what side of themselves they chose to give you?

That was entirely about them. You're not a mind reader. You're not a fortune-teller. And you most certainly aren't a psychologist. (Or maybe you are—but you're still reading this, aren't you?) So, you can't tell where the choices you make will take you. And you can't *predict* what lies beneath the surface of what people don't want to (or aren't prepared to) show you. And no, you also cannot predict where the people you meet will lead you. Or when. Or whether they'll be standing beside you three months from now. Or two years from now. Or there—in the end—for your lifetime. So please stop being so hard on yourself. You didn't know. You—can't—know. And it's ok. Because that's the way life goes. We all face hard truths. We all meet people we aren't ready for—who aren't ready for us. And we all learn something about ourselves in the process of losing the things we thought were ours to keep.

**

Experience is a funny thing, isn't it? I mean, so many people think that experience is what helps us make better decisions in the future. But— that's not just experience enabling that decision making, is it? Experience itself, I think, just gives us a past. It gives us a frame of reference. Graduates us to adulthood. Makes us tired. Frustrated. But not necessarily wiser. Because—we don't necessarily *learn anything* from experience itself, do we? We learn from *learning from* our experience. Evaluating it. Assessing how we responded to the new things that were placed in our path. And *changing* what didn't work (or we didn't like the outcome of) the next time.

Maybe you know one of those people who constantly repeats the same mistakes—and then asks you sincerely, "*why* does this keep happening to me?" Maybe you know one of those people who complain constantly about "not having the kind of life they want," but takes absolutely no steps in a direction that would actually change it. Maybe—maybe *you are* one of those people.

When we have any type of experience in this life—good or bad—it's our job to learn from it. Seriously. That is the *only* reason we get experience. To teach us. To help us shape how we *do* life in the future. Usually bad experiences are easier to learn from because—well, they hurt. And we *remember* hurt. We remember that when we do this, we feel that. And we did not like how that felt. So—we change. Quickly. Except, rather than really explore what it was that contributed to that being a bad experience for us, we often learn just the surface-level lessons. Avoidance—steer clear of things that hurt us. Or generalizations—all people respond to the same things in the same ways so watch for *that* in the future. Or worse—excuses. That's usually where we blame timing or the world or ourselves or the multitude of other insignificant or complicated things that can contribute in any way to giving us that experience.

Those aren't the lessons. The lessons aren't the bumper-sticker themes we extract from what we get in this life. The real lessons are—much deeper. Much more about *us*. And they take much more *time* to figure out.

**

So here's a question. *Did you like the person you were when you were with them?* What I mean is—did it feel good? Maybe the answer is yes. Maybe you liked how they made you feel. Maybe you liked how they added so significantly to your self-worth. How they built you up. Made you feel whole. Loved. Theirs. Or maybe—maybe you hated the person you were with them. Maybe you didn't feel the connection to your life that you used to. Maybe you neglected your family. Your friends. Your job. Your passions. You felt stagnant—stuck. But most likely, love, if you were to really think about it—you found yourself somewhere in the middle of those two places. Where part of you was better with them—but maybe you also lost a little of yourself in the process of becoming an us.

So what I want you to think about is whether you liked how they made you feel because you don't believe those things about yourself. I want you to really ask yourself—am I looking for someone to give me the confidence *I* don't have? Am I looking for someone to give me the life I can't give myself? Am I looking for someone to fill my bank account? To build my self-worth? To make me whole?

Because if any of those are even a little true—then you have some work to do before you can bring your best self forward into a healthy relationship in the future. And that growth happens with the questions. *Really digging* into the questions. Start with these:

How does what *I need* contribute to who *I pick*?

Do I always choose the same kind of people?

What is it that attracts me to them?

Do I give up what is important to me because I want *so badly* for someone to love me that I'm willing to do anything to get it?

The questions aren't the answer. But I promise you the simple act of reflecting on those questions is a big *part* of the answer. And *that* is something to build on.

**

Have you thought about what *you* need to learn from this? No, really. Whether you've decided, after all this thinking, that it was mainly your fault or mainly their fault or—*both* of your faults, this book wouldn't be complete without at least one section that is *entirely* about you. And what part you *could* have played in this. And I don't want it to sound the way I wrote it. I mean, it is *not* your fault when someone cheats on you. It is not *your* fault when someone blows up a relationship because of something they are struggling with. But—since it takes two people to make a relationship, perhaps—it takes two people to break one, too.

Stay with me here.

We all have baggage and layers and scars. We all have things that we *bring* to the table. Things that help a relationship grow—like our ability to communicate. Or be present. Or emotionally available. But we also have things that detract from a relationship, too—like our insecurities. Our fears. Our little hang-ups we've started to carry from the things that have happened to us in our lives. And while—none of those things *generally* can individually contribute to the complete downfall of a healthy relationship, they can certainly play their part.

I was in a relationship with someone who'd been cheated on in his past. He'd been married for the better part of a decade, and she'd cheated on him after all that time. He'd been overseas. She'd met *the guy* at the gym. Now, when I met him, he'd told me all this. He'd told me—honestly— that it had created some serious trust issues for him. We'd talked about what that meant. How it affected him. He was—*open* about the fact it was something he struggled with. A lot. And that made sense to me. Now, because he was talking to me about it and he seemed completely in touch with this part of himself, *I* thought that meant he was working through it. Getting past it. And the simple fact *we* could talk about it allowed me to rank it as something not *too important* on the red-flag scale. You know, that list you keep when you're just starting to get into a relationship? Where you track the things that have the potential to be bigger problems down the road?

Yeah. So—it was never an issue. Until—one night we went to a fitness class together. I had invited him to my studio, and the trainer who I'd known for—almost a year—stopped over to see how my workout was going. This was an instructor-led class, so it's not like he was sitting there engaging me in conversation. He just—checked in. Now guys—I'm telling you—we all have different personalities and *come across* in different ways. Sometimes people can interpret—or misinterpret—what we say and do. But I in *no way* crossed any boundaries. It was clear that I was there *with* someone. It was a *blip* on the radar that didn't even register on my scale until almost a week later when he had pulled away completely. And things eventually ended. When I went back and reflected on when and where the *energy* in the relationship had changed, it had been that moment. That completely insignificant (to me) moment when the trainer checked in on me and my workout. To him? To him—that was probably a shadow of his past he hadn't dealt with. One that broke us.

So that's what I mean.

I heard once that emotions can be like a temperature. They can spike quickly—but it takes a long time for them to go back down to normal. If we go into a relationship while our "temperature" is still high—then things like this situation happen. Or worse. And so your job, in every single experience you go through, is to figure out what that experience was trying to teach you. That goes for you as much as it goes for anyone that you end up with. And until you learn the lesson you needed to learn, you have no business carrying yourself into another classroom. Got it?

When you keep thinking the same way, you keep doing the same things. And when you keep doing the same things, you keep *getting* the same experiences. That makes sense, right? It's not enough to just know what you carry. It's about facing it. And then *working to deal with it* so that you take your healthiest self forward into your next chapter.

Because that's what *you* need.

And that's what *they* deserve.

**

At some point during your healing process, you have to start asking yourself some of the *really* hard questions. The ones we've just gone through are a good start—but you may need to ask yourself some others. Just what *those* questions are may vary depending on who you are and what you've been through. But there's one question that ties a lot of us together. Especially when we're searching for—getting—and then losing—our love stories.

Are you scared to be alone?

I mean, do you search for someone who is going to give you those pieces of yourself that always seem to be missing? And when *they* aren't there anymore, do you panic a little? Immediately feel that pressure of where you are and whether you're in the right place and—that you're *alone?*

It's ok. A lot of us do.

It's like you start to believe that if you don't keep moving forward as quickly as you can that whatever part of your past you're running from is going to catch up with you. And frankly—maybe that's exactly what you need. Maybe you *need it* to catch up with you so that you can make sense of it. Accept it. Learn something about what it was trying to teach you. And love? Maybe the past I'm talking about *isn't* this relationship. Or the last one. Maybe what you need to face came *way* before this. And you keep using each new relationship to avoid a part of you that you can't make sense of. A part that hurts too much *to try* to make sense of. But I'll tell you, there's a truth you probably need to face up to. And maybe you've never thought about it quite like this. But—let's explore it anyway.

When you are in pain—or you're really sick—you are naturally self-centered. Think about how it feels when you have a really bad headache. Or, maybe, the stomach virus. (I know, *not* a fun thing to imagine or remember). But—in both of those cases, you probably didn't go to work, right? Or school? You canceled on friends. Events. You didn't answer the phone. Or, if you did, you didn't get into long conversations. And it wasn't because, I'm guessing, you were worried about being *contagious.* It was because—you *didn't feel good.* And because you didn't feel *good,* you knew immediately that you weren't in the position to give *anything* else to *anyone* else.

Your needs came first.

Now, when you're sick, this isn't really a conscious choice. You don't have this thought process about how the choices you're making for you are going to affect others. You just know you can't give your best self, so you don't. You stay home until you're well. You put yourself first because you realize that *you* need you more than other people need you.

When you
keep thinking
the same way—
you keep doing
the same things.
And if you keep
doing the same things,
you keep getting the
same experiences.

So *that* is how you need to think about your emotional health, too. Self-centered people make self-centered decisions in relationships, right? And to be clear—what I mean is—when we're not emotionally *available* to ourselves—we cannot give a relationship with someone else what it needs to grow. And that's what I mean when I say—what did *you* need to learn from this?

While I was writing this chapter, I heard Jay Shetty say, "It's not about being *with* someone who makes you happy. It's about *being* someone who makes you happy." I know that's not your focus right now. But it should be. And it should be, soon. Because a big part of carrying your best self forward from here—is about knowing what you need to put down and *not* carry forward with you. A big part of what you need to learn from this is *who* this experience will make you. How much it will change you. And I promise you, no matter how you feel about whether you need to be your best self *before* you meet your one or whether you guys can figure that out together—you *always* have to be working on who you are and what you're bringing to the relationship.

People bring out different parts of us. And maybe that's the purpose for all the people we cross paths with in this life that we can't quite under-stand. Maybe they are there to show us how to make our own hearts strong and our own eyes clear. Maybe they are there to hold our hands long enough for us to set down the heavy things we've been carrying. Or maybe—maybe they are there to show us how *much* we can love some-one. I like to think that if I loved the wrong people that much—I've got *a heck of a lot* to give to the right one. Maybe that will comfort you, too.

So look, love. As much as you don't want to right now, *use* this experi-ence. Grow from it. In whatever way you can. Take some time to explore who you are now, with this experience as part of your journey. And get your heart healthy. Get your head healthy. Because when you are healthy—when your heart and your mind are ready, and willing, and able to contribute to being with someone else—you face love with clarity. And clarity is an incredible foundation to build upon. So—what part of this situation was yours? Even if it was mostly about them, *what part of this* is something you could focus on? Grow from?

I've become very convinced in my life that our experiences are split down the middle in regard to what we're supposed to learn from them. I think that *half* the time, we're getting the experience so we can learn something about the world. And the other half? So the world can teach us something about *ourselves.*

Maybe this had to happen because *you* needed to learn something about *you.*

Do you know what it was yet?

**

It's almost time to wrap this book up. And I have just one last thing to tell you.

Life *is* going to give you what you need. I promise you it will.

I know the crazy roads this life takes us on feel anything but purposeful. But *everything* you get in this life has the potential to give you more than you had without it. These times where we go through the hard stuff? Where we lose people and things that mattered to us? Where we fight our hearts and our minds to make sense of chaos? They are *all* opportunities. To learn something about our lives. Ourselves. What we need. Want. Want to be.

A big part
of carrying your
best self forward
is about knowing
what **you do *not* need**
to carry forward.

One day you're going to get the things you've been waiting for. One day it *will* be your turn. And when that day comes, you are going to understand why you had to go through what you went through. All the questions are going to be answered—the endings understood. The knots you've tied yourself into will come undone—the tension in your shoulders will dissipate. Your heart will be whole. And stronger for all that it has navigated with you. The trick to this whole loving thing is just figuring out how to get through these hard times. And then come out better for having done it.

So—love a lot. Love *a lot*. And whatever you do, just never let anything— or anyone—scare you away from opening up your heart the next time.

Your story is far from over, love.

And remember. If things aren't ok yet—this was not the end.

**

Epilogue: "What I Was Supposed to Learn from This."

Some final thoughts to take with you.

I heard once that 70 percent of us are hanging on to "the one that got away." Now, I don't know if that's exactly true or not—but it got me thinking. It got me thinking about all the reasons that relationships end.

Or never really start in the first place.

I mean, it could be timing. Like, you and that other person are just not standing in the same place at the same time. Or maybe you don't want the same things. Or maybe you have dreams that take you in opposite directions and it just happened naturally. Or maybe you couldn't trust them. Or they couldn't trust you. Maybe there was something unhealthy that forced you to part ways. Maybe—and this may be the hardest one to understand of them all—there was no reason at all. At least not one you understand right now. But whatever the case may be, you have to do some really careful balancing between the movie version of hanging on to your long-lost love—and the reality that holding on to the past makes it *really* difficult to walk into the future.

I don't know how long you're going to hold on to the person who made you read this book. Only you know that. And I am definitely not saying you should give up on something that really matters to you. Or someone you can't go a day without thinking about. [Although, in fairness, right now your mind and heart *aren't* being fair to you. That's why time is better for you than the wars happening between what you *think* and what you *feel*.]

What I am saying, though, is while you're figuring it all out—don't stand still. Don't stop and wait for them to catch up—to find you. To call you. To apologize. To change. To heal. To grow. Trust me when I say if it is *meant to happen*, this universe will find a way to bring the two of you back together. Trust me on that one.

**

Ok. So what you really want to know is how someone can walk away when nothing was broken. Or hard. When—heck, it was straight-up incredible. No red flags. No warning signs. No bad stuff. You want to know how someone can cheat on you when you gave them everything. When they promised everything. When it took you *both so long* to build it, but only seconds to destroy it. You want to know how someone that promised you the world and talked about forever could become someone who transitions so quickly into words of *never*. This is *never* going to work. We can *never* work through this. You want to know how someone that was once your everything can now wear a face you no longer recognize. In your mind, you think knowing the why will calm your racing thoughts—will heal the cracks they drove so unexpectedly into your heart. "Why" would be a loose end you could tie up, right? One that would let you move on. Heal. Start over. I know.

But here's the thing. Love—it looks like so much more than just an empty space beside you. It looks like so much more than someone who isn't willing to work through this life with you. Or can't. And you know this one already, but I'll say it anyway—love looks like so much more than you doing it all for the both of you. Especially when things get real. I know you think understanding will help you to heal, but you know we don't always get the answers at the same time we ask the questions. Sometimes we just have to trust the most fundamental truths there are. And this one—this one is a big one.

Love is not footsteps walking away from you. It's not you crying all alone. It's not someone who runs hot and cold. Who turns on a dime. Who flips a switch and burns it all down. Love is not questions about whether they love you or where they are or whether they're telling you the truth. And no matter what the reason is, or was, it's time to accept what you already know is true.

You do *not* want someone who has to walk away. For *any* reason.

Because love is steady. And sure. And open—you hear me? Open. So just remember, that even with that head full of questions you may never get an answer to—or at least not right now—that one thing will always be true.

Love stays. If it's real, it stays. Even when (especially when) it's hard.

**

I get that this whole *love* thing is taking so much longer than you want it to—than you expected it to. I get that you are going to have questions and insecurities and baggage and scars. But I also need you to get this. This single, beautifully complex, imperfectly perfect truth that I already told you about a few chapters back. But I am going to tell you again. Because it's *that* important:

Love is not about finding someone who knows how to love you perfectly.

It's about finding someone who wants to try.

Make sure you get that right. I mean it. Make sure you eventually start asking yourself why you run after the things that run from you. Make sure you eventually ask yourself why you would even *want* to build a life with someone you can't talk to. Or don't open up to. Or can't trust. Or doesn't listen. Or—who doesn't want to know the parts of you that aren't shiny.

Because love isn't always shiny.

The heart is a lot like a sponge. And so the *most important choice* you will ever make in this life is which voices you let soak into it. Which voices— which experiences—which lessons—you sew into the fibers of who you are and call your story. You *become* the sum of what you choose to keep in your life. And that choice is yours. Right now.

Sure. This whole thing might have happened *to* you. It might not have been something you had control over. Something you planned. Something you—wanted. But it did. And the choice you need to make is whether this whole thing that happened *to* you is something that you let *become* you.

*

The truth is, I don't want to be good at this phase. The untangling. Because being good at it means I have to perfect the art of doing it— which also means I have to go through it. Enough to have the experience of actually *getting* good at it. So, even though I don't want to be good at it—I do want to get to a place where I know myself. And what is healthy for me. And that goes with people and scenarios and every single thing in-between.

I've been through this a few times now—and while I never expected it to get easier, in some ways it has. I don't actually think that has anything to do with the situation. But rather, how I have taught myself to respond to it. Somewhere along the line, I've started to accept endings for what they are. You've heard me say that a few times now. Commas. Or periods. But in either case—places I need to pause and think about what this life is trying to teach me.

It's not the situations that have gotten better. It's me.

And I'm not joking, guys. Endings hurt. I'm there. And I still have a lot of soul searching to do. A lot of missing what was—what was going to be. But because I'm a writer, I heal by writing. That's another fundamental truth I have come to accept. I write what hurts. And this—hurt. I always hope that what I write, especially when it's hard—will find its way into your heart and help you heal, too. And from what you tell me every day on Instagram, it does.

**

The morning after the breakup that caused this book, I remember asking over and over—"what am I supposed to learn from this?" In my mind, things had been good. In my mind, there was absolutely nothing wrong.

No red flags. No warning signs. No hot and cold. He wanted to plan things—he wanted—an us. Or at least he said so. He made me trust him because he told me I could. And then he *seemed like* he could prove it. At least, right up until the end. When I looked at a stranger where the person I knew used to be. The person that, days before, was the one telling me—I'm here. I want to be here. I will be here.

So like I said, the question I asked over and over and over in those first few days was *what am I supposed to learn from this?* In the depths of heartache, I remember answering my own question out loud. *Maybe I'm supposed to learn that I can't trust anyone. Maybe I'm supposed to learn that even people that awaken those special parts of you can also rip what they plant right out of you, too.* But then I pulled myself together and I got my head and my heart focused on *the lesson*. Because, like I hope I've convinced you, there *always* is one. Always. And for the life of me, I will never know why that man treated me the way he did at the end. But maybe that's his story. And not mine. Because through this journey, even though it was a short one, I learned the lesson that this life wanted me to learn. And I understand it now.

I am a writer. You've known that for a long time. And I—I've known it my whole life. I had a plan for book two. I wanted it to come fairly quickly after *Courage to Rise*. So I worked to get the manuscript written. And it—*is*—written. On my computer. Where it has sat. Since the week *before* Courage to Rise officially came out. Waiting to be edited.

At the time, I didn't know what it was that was preventing me from spending the time I knew it would take to get that book ready for you. At the time, I blamed it on how busy my life was, how complicated things were. But when it came right down to it, the truth was—my heart just wasn't in that story. At least for now.

And now I know why.

I couldn't finish book two for you because *that* was not book two. The reason that I had to go through what I went through with this person was because *this* is my story. At least for right now. This is the story that I needed to write. For you. For me. For every single one of us that is piecing together the parts of our hearts that someone else got to hold for a while. For every single one of us that knows what it feels like to let go of someone—and something—they love most. For every single one of us struggling to see the answers in the aftermath of a love story.

This was the book I needed to write.

And the *reason* all this happened—that *he* was part of my story—is actually quite simple, too. And maybe, now, in some ways quite perfect. Some people are meant to be *pieces* of chapters in our lives. Other people are meant to take whole chapters up, all on their own. And yes, *sometimes* other people just make choices for *them* that end up making choices for *us*.

And that is the beauty of how this life works. How little we know about what we actually need. How *much* we want to control everything, plan everything. And how wonderful it is, truly, when we see things come together we never knew we even needed in the first place.

His job was not to *be* the story.

His job was to make me *see* the story.

And my job—*my job* was simply, to write it.

**

Moving Forward Together

Thank you for finding this book. And for reading it. And for making it *all* the way here to the last few pages. And thank you *even more* for taking this journey with me—for being open to something different—for allowing me to join you on those first few beautifully difficult steps. **If you want to know a little more about what ended up happening with my story *after* writing this book, be sure to check out the acknowledgments section.**

I hope you've come through this book with a heart that's a little stronger. A little surer. Maybe—one that is full of a little more hope for tomorrow. Just know it's a long journey back to your own heart. And it takes time. Go easy on yourself, love. *Go easy.*

And just so you know, there is *so much more* where this came from. *Courage to Rise,* my first book, is a great place to start—please check it out if you want to read more. If you'd like to *hear* more, check out *Life Letters,* my new podcast. It's available on Apple, Spotify, iHeartRadio, Google, and a large number of your other favorite sites. And it's my way of bringing words to life.

I write every single day. I've been doing it most of my life, but just recently started my book and social media journey. I put my words out there daily because I hope—with everything that I am—that they will find the heart that is looking for them. I write in the hopes that reading my words might help other people as much as it has helped me to write them. But mostly—I write in the hopes we can all help each other a little on this crazy beautiful journey called life.

I'd love to hear your story. Or what you thought of this book. Please reach out on Instagram. Or Facebook. Or feel free to shoot me an email. I always do my best to respond personally.

Oh—and if you liked this book, I'd be so incredibly honored if you'd be willing to review it. On Amazon. Or Barnes and Noble. Or Goodreads. Or any other site you might see *Untangling* being sold. Authors really need (and value) that feedback—and I would absolutely love to hear from you. Contact me:

On Social Media: @liveinthedetails on Instagram, Facebook, and Tumblr, @emmagraceauthor on Twitter.

Via the Web: www.liveinthedetails.com

By Email: liveinthedetails@gmail.com

Acknowledgments

I don't think a writer writes the stories they *want* to write. A writer writes the stories that *want* to be written. That *need* to be written. That choose *them*.

And for a million different reasons, for this chapter of my life, this story was mine.

As with most books, while the author may type the actual words, there are *so many people* that make it possible for the story to come together into what we can call a *book*. The tidbits of conversations that weave themselves into pages—and then chapters. The influence of people who dole out those incredible nuggets of wisdom that get all wrapped up in how a mind thinks and a heart processes. The kindhearted friends and family, with their endless patience and perspective and love. But mostly, the confidence and stability and security that a writer draws upon from those people who stand by them. Consistently. Unwavering. Through it all.

I am so incredibly blessed to have the people in my life that I do. And even in writing a book about—in its most bumper-sticker roll-up—*loss,*

A few days ago, as my father was walking me to my car, he stopped as he opened the door and looked quietly at me. "You know," he said gently, "You changed my life." I looked up at him, surprised, and he continued. "Men who don't have daughters will never understand how significantly they change a man's life. But they do. *You* did." Those words will stay with me. I know we haven't always understood each other—haven't always agreed—but I also know your choices *have always* been made from a place of what you believed was best for me. And I want you to know—I do remember the moments. The garden in the morning. The camping. The salamanders. The hunt to find crystals. Flying kites. Roasting apples on sticks. Building igloos. Tree forts. Life doesn't always go as planned, and I know this has been a hard year for you. For all of us. I don't know what time has in store, or what will happen over the coming months and years. But I want to thank you for always being the one out front. For fighting the battles. For worrying about the things we never had to think about. For giving us opportunities. And mostly—for building, and then rebuilding, the foundation that we all built our lives from. I know you gave up a lot so that so we could be who we are. It wasn't perfect, but it was ours. So thank you for being the person you never knew you were going to be. So that I could, too.

As I write this section, I am finding myself willing and ready to take a risk in writing what I am about to write. Shortly after I finished this book, I met the person who made everything I had to go through to get here *worth* it. And you know, I don't know what the future holds there, either. I don't know where he and I will be when this book is published and he reads these words. And I certainly don't know if time will tell a story where he and I are together in the end (although I certainly hope it does). But as with all love stories, that's the risk. That is *always* the risk. And so, regardless of what happens from when I write these words to the time this book is published, I want him to know that either way, every single moment was worth it. Sometimes we overuse the word amazing these days—but in this case, I mean it with the absolute perfection in its original definition. I posted something on Instagram the other day that I had written almost a year ago. I write a lot about how I hope the world (my world) will one day be. Little did I know, this ended up being you. "*When you meet your person, you know. You are simply—content—in the beautifully simple truth that the world is big and life is good and time was right.*"

And lastly, I want to thank the person who caused me to write this book. At the time, I didn't understand why you were put in my path—but I do now. I do because while I will never be grateful for the experience—I was, and am, grateful for the opportunity. For people like you to be put in my path, and in doing so, to teach me *what I want* by learning well *what I do not.* For giving me the catalyst to write the story I needed to write. For me. For you. For every single one of us that is piecing together a heart in the aftermath of a love story. Shortly after I finished this book, he texted me. It was about six months after he last left me standing on that curb. And the message—not an apology. Just a hello. An "I'm thinking of you but don't expect you to respond." I didn't. But you know, that message wasn't meant to open a door. Or start a conversation. Or revisit a chapter. That message was simply proof that time does know **exactly** what it is doing. And that our unanswered prayers—our *nos*—our *you're-not-the-ones*—are sometimes the best things we have never wanted for our lives. Like I said, he wasn't the story. But he awoke the story in me that needed to be written. And so, maybe in the end it goes something like this. Life is just an imperfectly perfect kaleidoscope of pieces that fall into place in a million different ways—and this was just his piece in the big, beautiful mess of colors that are constantly forming my picture. He was the ending that created a beginning. An incredible one. One that—without having experienced what I did and feeling what I felt and writing what I wrote—I would never have had eyes to see.

And eyes—*eyes*— are what experience is all about.

**

The rest of my thank-yous—in no particular order—need to go to these beautiful souls:

My writing inspiration for the past *twenty years,* Kimberly Kirberger. Thank you for believing in me when I was just starting out. And for believing in me, still, when I finally had the courage to write my first book. Thank you for your guidance, your advocacy, your friendship, and mostly, your time. It means more than you know.

For Jack Canfield, the man with the dream who created the series that elevated my love of writing. Your story—your perseverance— are what enabled me, and so many of us, to share the dream of being published writers right beside you. Thank you for the chance. And for your continued support of one girl's big dream.

My best friend Lindsey, to whom this book is dedicated, and whose never-ending patience and wisdom and love have been a guiding force in my life. You are the truest definition of a forever friend. Neither time nor geography nor life's chaos has been able to erase what we have drawn into this life. Thank you for being my person.

My friend Stephanie for the words she shared with me years ago—about how *I had the power to control how I felt about things*. While we haven't talked in years, and I truly didn't understand the gravity of what they meant back then—I do now. Very much. And that very small excerpt from one very small conversation from long ago in the past—has echoed in my head ever since. And changed me.

My incredible life coach, Julie. For your experience, your guidance, and mostly, for your deep well of sage advice that just *never* seems to dry up. You show so many of us how to steer our way through this life. Thank you for being the light in the darkness that helps us find our way.

Heidi Priebe, for her kindness in letting me sprinkle her amazing words of wisdom throughout this book.

For Andy Stanley, for being a constant source of inspiration each morning with his amazing podcast *Your Move.*

My oh-so-talented editor, Katherine Rawson.

And my publisher, Morgan James.

About the Author

Emma Grace is the author behind the hugely popular series *Live in the Details.* Following the release of her first book, *Courage to Rise,* in December 2018, Emma has risen in popularity, with millions flocking weekly to Instagram and Facebook to read her words—and thousands flocking weekly to her new podcast, *Life Letters,* on Apple, Spotify, iHeartRadio and Google.

Known as the author who *finds* the words to talk about the things that are *hardest* to talk about, Emma brings the conversational tone of a good friend to the wisdom of an old one. She writes about life. And love. And growth. And the spectrum of other things that fall in-between. Her words capture readers *where they are* and walk them, gently, through the hugely complicated kaleidoscope of experiences that are this life.

Emma's words are raw, real, and honest. Her stream of consciousness style captures in a simple, yet beautiful way, all the things that people see and feel and are. She is a believer. In taking risks. In trusting. In every-thing happens for a reason. But mostly—in big love and the power of one person to change their little corner of this world. So as long as she is breathing—that is what you will find her doing.

Originally from the Hudson Valley in upstate New York, Emma now lives in Arlington, Virginia, just outside of Washington, DC, with a busy consulting career alongside her writing.